BRIEF INTRODUCTION TO THE STUDY OF THEOLOGY

Notre Dame Studies in Theology
Volume 1

Lawrence S. Cunningham, *general editor*

Brief Introduction to the Study of Theology

with Reference to the Scientific Standpoint and the Catholic System

JOHANN SEBASTIAN DREY

Translated with an Introduction
and Annotation by MICHAEL J. HIMES

UNIVERSITY OF NOTRE DAME PRESS
Notre Dame   London

Copyright © 1994 by
University of Notre Dame Press
Notre Dame, Indiana 46556
All Rights Reserved
Manufactured in the United States of America

Library of Congress Cataloging-in-Publication Data

Drey, Johann Sebastian von, 1777–1853.
  [Kurze Einleitung in das Studium der Theologie.   English]
  Brief introduction to the study of theology : with reference to
the scientific standpoint and the Catholic system / by Johann
Sebastian Drey ; translated by Michael J. Himes.
    p.   cm. — (Notre Dame studies in theology ; v. 1)
  ISBN 0-268-01171-0
  1. Theology—Study and teaching—Catholic Church.
2. Theology—Study and teaching—Germany—Tübingen.
3. Catholic Church—Doctrines.   4. Tübingen School (Catholic
theology)   I. Title. II. Series.
BX895.D7413   1994
230' .2—dc20   93-42343
                                                           CIP

∞ *The paper used in this publication meets the minimum requirements
of the American National Standard for Information Sciences— Permanence of Paper
for Printed Library Materials,* ANSI Z39.48-1984.

CONTENTS

Acknowledgments vii
Introduction ix
    BRIEF INTRODUCTION TO THE STUDY OF THEOLOGY
Foreword xxxiii
    PART ONE: General Information
    Section One: Religion—Revelation—Christianity
I. Religion 1
II. Revelation 7
III. Christianity 12
    Section Two: Theology—Specifically Christian Theology
[I. General Meaning of Theology] 16
II. Christian Theology 20
III. Scope, Content, and Organization of Theology 24
IV. Theological Encyclopedia 32
    Section Three: Presuppositions of Theological Study 39
    PART TWO: Encyclopedic Outline of
    the Major Branches of Theological Studies
I. Historical Propaedeutic
  A.1. Biblical Study 51
      Method of Biblical Study 57
  A.2. Exegesis 59
    a) History of Biblical Texts 60
    b) Biblical Criticism 66
    c) Biblical Philology 68
    d) Biblical Hermeneutics 71
      Method of Exegetical Study 76
  B. Historical Theology 80

B.1. External History of Christianity	83
B.2. Internal History of Christianity	87
B.3. Sources of Church History	93
B.4. Study and Method of Historical Theology	98
II. Scientific Theology	
A. Foundational Studies	102
A.1. Apologetics	105
A.2. Polemics	109
B. Specialized Science	113
B.1. System of Christian Doctrine	116
B.2. System of the Christian Church	124
B.3. Study of Scientific Theology	142
III. Practical Theology	149
1. Introduction to Church Government	153
2. Introduction to Church Administration or to Church Ministry	162
3. Study of Practical Theology	171
Translator's Notes	177
Selected Bibliography	181

ACKNOWLEDGMENTS

The nineteenth-century Catholic theologians at Tübingen have continued to interest me in the fifteen years since I did my dissertation on J. A. Möhler at the Divinity School of the University of Chicago. The lack of English translations of their work has been a problem for those who teach the history of nineteenth-century theology to students who are not "at home" in German. I have long thought that Drey's encyclopedic introduction to theology for his students is an especially helpful primary text for those today who want to discover the remarkably rich theological work done in German Catholic circles at the beginning of the 1800s. But the translation would not have been done had it not been for a deeply appreciated sabbatical semester granted me by the Department of Theology and the College of Arts and Letters of the University of Notre Dame. During that semester I was made welcome by Monsignor John Strynkowski and the faculty and staff of the Seminary of the Immaculate Conception, Huntington, New York; it is a pleasure to acknowledge their hospitality. I also thank my cousins Virginia and Edward Sermier, who graciously made available to me Stone Acres, their home in the Pocono Mountains. My research assistant, Mr. Thomas Poundstone, generously put his scholarly skills to work in tracking down some of Drey's more obscure references; I owe him thanks for many acts of kindness. I am indebted to my colleagues Professors Lawrence Cunningham and Thomas O'Meara, O.P., for their reading of the introduction and text and their wise suggestions. Mr. James Langford, Director of the University of Notre Dame Press, provided encouragement by asking me to submit the translation to the Press even before it was begun and saw it through the process of its publication. Thus, for the time, the place, and the assistance, I am most grateful.

    I am delighted to have this opportunity to express gratitude for gifts extending back many years by dedicating this translation to the memory of four old friends and mentors: Vincent J. Powell, John J. Gorman, Edward W. Offenheiser, and Henry J. Zimmer. Their company was a privilege; their example remains with me.

INTRODUCTION

Almost two decades ago a history of Catholic theology in the nineteenth century concluded that only two of the theological systems elaborated in that century were still vital in the last quarter of the twentieth century, neo-Thomism, because it had unwittingly laid the foundation for the transcendental Thomism of Karl Rahner and Bernard Lonergan, and "Drey's Tübingen theology."[1] The Catholic Tübingen school's emphasis on history, its theology of tradition and doctrinal development, and its concern with ecclesiology as part of the mystery of faith have taken deep root in Catholic theology. The theological approaches and concerns which the Catholic faculty at Tübingen brought to the fore marked an important moment in the history of modern Catholic thought. Thomas O'Meara has demonstrated that the theologians of the first half of the nineteenth century in Germany staked out a position for dialogue with the major intellectual currents of their time.[2] Their work clearly showed that Catholic thought could open itself without fear to modernity and profit from the experience. That openness was sufficiently rare in Catholic theological circles that even at the beginning of this century there were those who charged the Catholic Tübingen school with being the most likely candidate as the ancestor of modernism.[3]

But why "*Drey's* Tübingen theology"? Johann Sebastian Drey, the most important member of the first generation of the Catholic faculty at Tübingen and the teacher of the other prominent members of the school, has remained largely unknown to the English-speaking world. Nearly twenty years after the judgment quoted above regarding the continuing importance of the Catholic Tübingen school and Drey's central role in it, nearly a century and a half after his death, none of his work, with the exception of one early article, has been translated into English. The best introduction to Drey's theology—indeed, as a programmatic work, the best introduction to the Catholic Tübingen school as a whole—is his *Kurze Einleitung in das Studium der Theologie mit Rücksicht auf den Wissenschaftlichen Standpunkt und das katholische System*, Short Introduction to the Study of Theology with Reference to the Scientific Standpoint and the Catholic System.[4]

THE FATHER OF THE CATHOLIC TÜBINGEN SCHOOL

Johann Sebastian Drey[5] was born into poverty in the village of Killingen on October 16, 1777. Killingen was in the territory of the counts of Ottingen, one of many small principalities between the Catholic Kingdom of Bavaria and the predominantly Lutheran Duchy of Württemberg. From the age of ten Drey received a far better education than the poverty of his family could ever have provided. The local pastor, Martin Ziegler, a Jesuit until the suppression of the Society of Jesus in 1773 and a man of considerable theological education, recognized the boy's intellectual gifts and sent him to the *Gymnasium* in nearby Ellwangen. There he was supported by donations from local people until, after a few years, he could earn some money by tutoring. The young student found great pleasure in theology, classical languages, mathematics, and the natural sciences. Having finished his basic studies at the *Gymnasium* and more advanced classes at the *Lyzeum*, in 1797 he moved to Augsburg, where for the next two years he supported himself as a tutor in the home of a customs agent in Wertach-Brücke. After two years he entered the Augsburg diocesan seminary at Pfaffenhausen. Having been ordained in 1801, he became vicar of his home parish of Röhlingen and an assistant to his benefactor, Ziegler. During the next five years, Drey continued the wide reading which he had begun in his student days in contemporary philosophy, especially Kant, Fichte, Jacobi, and Schelling.

These personal studies received a new direction from the new pastor of Röhlingen, Johann Nepomuk Bestlin, who succeeded Ziegler in 1805. Bestlin had been the favorite pupil of Johann Michael Sailer, at that time an immensely influential teacher at Ingolstadt, later to be bishop of Regensburg, and often regarded as the "father" of the Catholic revival in southern Germany in the first half of the nineteenth century. Bestlin had been part of the circle of bright young men around Sailer, many of whom became teachers of theology or bishops and exerted a profound influence on the course of Catholic life in Germany. He was an advocate of reform in church structure and liturgy and was eager to see reform come from within the church rather than as an imposition by civil government. As a disciple of Sailer, Bestlin was deeply interested in the Catholic mystical tradition, and that interest was passed on to his young assistant at Röhlingen. Thus, through Bestlin, Drey came into contact with those proposing internal church reforms and began to combine a wider sense of the richness of the Catholic theological tradition with his study of contemporary philosophy. But Drey's life as a parish priest did not last long. In 1806 he took the position of instructor in religious philosophy, mathematics, and physics at the Catholic *Lyzeum* in Rottweil in the new Kingdom of Württemberg.

In the years between 1803 and 1806, the political contours of Drey's world had changed dramatically. Napoleon absorbed into his French empire the lands west of the Rhine and shifted and combined the numerous German principalities east of the river. Württemberg had profited by having various of its neighbors annexed to it and being elevated to the status of a kingdom. Much of the old county of Ottingen, where Drey had been born, was now part of the new kingdom. Württemberg, a largely Lutheran territory under the rule of Catholic dukes, now contained within its borders a large Catholic minority which the new government set out to attach to the regime. One of the ways it attempted to do this was by expanding the Catholic educational center at Ellwangen into a seminary with university status in 1812. To this new *Friedrichslandesuniversität* Drey was called as professor of dogmatics, history of dogma, apologetics, and theological encyclopedia. The elevated status and impressive name of the new seminary did not make up for the paucity of resources. It did, however, number several energetic and talented scholars on its faculty, among them Drey's former pastor Bestlin, now professor of moral and pastoral theology and a major influence on the plan of studies at Ellwangen. But Drey soon allied himself with the professor of New Testament studies, Peter Alois Gratz, another Sailer student and advocate of church reform, in opposing Bestlin on one important question: whether the new faculty should stay at Ellwangen or seek to join the long-established university of Tübingen. Eventually the counsel of Gratz and Drey prevailed on the Württemberg government. Accepting their complaints about the inadequacy of library resources at the new institution and their concerns that Catholic clergy educated in an exclusively Catholic area such as Ellwangen might become sectarian and interfere with the official policy of religious toleration, the government moved the theological faculty to Tübingen in 1817. Tübingen thus became a university with two theology faculties, Catholic and Protestant.

During his years of teaching at Ellwangen, Drey had been engaged in a careful reading of contemporary philosophy, especially that of Schelling, and theology, especially that of Schleiermacher. The direction of his thought can be seen from an essay which he published in 1812 in which he called for the renewal of Catholic theology.[6] Medieval theology had been a wonderful, if sometimes naive synthesis of life and thought in which scholastic theology raised to reflection the communal life of the Christian church. But that period had been followed by the arid word games of decadent scholasticism, which had in turn alienated from theology both the mystical and intuitive element of Christian life and genuine philosophy. The Reformers had attempted to base their theology on the texts of scripture but in doing so opened the way for theology to be replaced by philology. They also made the individual hearer's or reader's relation to the text the center of theological consideration rather than the community's Spirit-directed life. Left to themselves, mysticism became increasingly individualistic and bizarre, and philosophy ended in materialism and skepticism. Catholic theologians had attempted to respond to Protestantism by expanding the array of relevant texts to include the Fathers of the church and hierarchical decrees but otherwise accepted the assumption that theology was argument about the interpretation of the past, not a reflection on the life present in the community. Thus theology had come to the sad state in which it languished at the beginning of the nineteenth century.

But the claim that theology is the reflection of the life of the community does not mean that the theologian becomes an ecclesiastical propagandist who seeks to justify whatever the church does. Reflection rooted in the on-going historical life of the community may well uncover distortions of that life, deformities, false claims, and mistaken practices. Thus, in 1815, in a study of the origins of private confession, Drey concluded that not only was the practice not instituted by Christ as the Council of Trent had taught, it was not even apostolically instituted.[7] What is more noteworthy, however, is that Drey did not think that this disqualified private confession as a true and vital part of the church's penitential discipline. For the objective element in theology is not the dead letter of ecclesiastical documents but unfolding tradition, a "natural process of causation which the Holy Spirit uses as the preparation for development of new dogmas."[8]

To foster the development of a contemporary Catholic theology in Germany, in 1819, the same year in which he published his *Brief Introduction to the Study of Theology*, Drey founded with several colleagues in the Catholic theological faculty the *Theologische Quartalschrift*, which remains today the oldest continually published journal for Catholic theology and to which he devoted much time as an editor and writer.

Drey remained at Tübingen for the rest of his life. He declined a call to the chair of dogmatic theology at the university of Freiburg in 1821, the university which had awarded him a doctorate in theology in 1814. In 1822 his name was put forward for the bishopric of Rottenburg by the Württemberg government, but he was rejected by Rome, in part because of the opinions he had expressed in his monograph on private confession and even more because he had subscribed to the declaration of the Frankfurt Conference in 1818. That document had been the product of a meeting of various German principalities, headed by the government of Württemberg, which had set forth principles for church-state relations and had been rejected by the Vatican. Eventually, in 1827, Rome did accede to a compromise measure which effectively recognized the right of the governments of the German states and the cathedral chapters of various dioceses to appoint bishops. But in 1822 Drey's advocacy of the Frankfurt Conference statement was ample reason for Rome to reject his candidacy.[9]

In 1837 Drey's health, weakened by the deprivations due to his straitened circumstances during his student years, began to fail. As a result he surrendered his responsibility to lecture on dogmatic theology and concentrated on apologetics and theological encyclopedia until his retirement in 1846. His severe illness spurred Drey to begin publishing the major work on which he had been laboring for some years, his apologetics, which appeared in three volumes.[10] He remained intellectually active after his retirement from teaching and was a frequent book reviewer for the *Theologische Quartalschrift* during his last years. He died of a sudden stroke on February 19, 1853. Besides his published works,[11] he left his lecture notes in dogmatics,[12] the texts of his lectures on the history of doctrine in the first three centuries,[13] and his journals.[14] In addition to his scholarly work, throughout the forty years of his teaching career—six at Rottweil, five at Ellwangen, and twenty-nine at Tübingen—he had been active in practical issues of liturgical and pastoral reform. But perhaps his greatest influence came through his students, F. A. Staudenmaier, J. E. Kuhn, K. J. Hefele, and especially J. A. Möhler.[15]

A Theological Encyclopedia

In form, Drey's *Brief Introduction to the Study of Theology* is, as he himself described it, a "theological encyclopedia." In eighteenth- and nineteenth-century Germany, "encyclopedia" did not mean what is ordinarily meant by the term in English today. Our contemporary use of the term is much closer to what Diderot and d'Alembert intended their famous *encyclopédie* to be: a compendium of articles which would provide the intelligent reader necessary knowledge on subjects other than those in which one had professional expertise. By contrast, Drey and his German contemporaries used the term to designate an overview of a field or discipline in which the reader was assumed to be professionally interested. The expansion of fields within theology in the course of the eighteenth century—due to the emergence of critical biblical exegesis, textual criticism, new methods in church history, etc.—made pressing the need for a systematic laying out of the branches of theology and the methods employed in them, and several writers, Catholic and Protestant, responded by supplying theological encyclopedias. In the Foreword to his theological encyclopedia, Drey wrote of the "formal and material" aspects of an encyclopedia (p. 4). By the material aspect he meant the requirement of introducing students into the history of theology so that they might be made familiar with terminology, standard references, and perennial questions and of explaining the methods and resources available for students of the discipline. But it quickly becomes apparent that this material aspect is subordinate to the formal aspect in which Drey was much more interested. The material information will be of little use and less interest to a student, he maintained, unless the student can see how the discipline as a whole relates to other fields of knowledge and how the various subdisciplines relate to and affect one another. This is why the first part of the book is given over to a "thoroughgoing deduction" (p. 3) of the key concepts which are at play in Christian theology and why the second part is so concerned with the correct order of study of the subdisciplines. Unless and until these "formal" considerations were clear,

Drey held that the history of the field and bibliographical suggestions were inappropriate and, in fact, aside from a very few passing references, he did not supply the reader of his *Brief Introduction* with these. In Drey's own terms, the book is ruled by "formal" considerations.

History, Hermeneutics and Science

According to #107 of the *Brief Introduction*, "the most common and the primary way" to treat Christianity is "as a temporal phenomenon." Drey immediately noted that this can be interpreted in two ways: one can think of Christianity as "one moment in the general history of religion" or as a unique historical whole in and of itself. The former is a helpful, perhaps necessary perspective for the Christian theologian, but the latter is the specific way of regarding Christianity which is proper to theology. Thus, Drey stated, the theologian understands Christianity "as the center of all historical religious phenomena." The study of Christianity understood in this way in "a purely historical fashion" is historical theology, for Drey a very important area within theology as a whole.

The first way of treating Christianity as a historical phenomenon—as one moment within the religious history of humanity—was the usual perspective of the Enlightenment. Christianity could then be seen as one historically conditioned form of "natural religion," those fundamental truths which underlay all religious traditions and confessions although sometimes obscured or distorted by the particular historical forms—doctrines, rituals, codes of conduct, etc.—in which various religions have expressed them. Thus, in the title of a famous eighteenth-century Deist tract, Christianity is "as old as the creation," and the Gospel is simply "a republication of the religion of nature."[16] And, it should be noticed, the Gospel is *a* republication of natural religion, not *the* republication, for whatever it contains of truth is the valuable content of every other religion as well. While certainly not agreeing that this "natural religion" is the sole content of any value in Christianity nor accepting the claim that at base Christianity is the same as every other religion, Drey did acknowledge the "philosophical meaning of Christianity." That meaning, which is "in continuity with previous revelations," is the realization by humanity, which has "been educated by God in numerous ways," of its true situation in the universe and before God, i.e., its utter dependence upon God and the destructive madness of trying to assert independence from God (#29). This is the truth of what Drey called "natural revelation," which is, in this respect, the only revelation, for "there is nothing which can be revealed by God to man save in man or in nature, and there is nothing which is without relevance to his or its relation to God" (#17). Thus, there is a sense in which true religion is as old as the creation, for "as with religion, revelation has been from the beginning, continues in the present, and can never come to an end" (#16). Nevertheless, although various people may have anticipated the full unfolding of this natural revelation in their heartfelt longing for redemption from the mad striving for independence from God, the historical event of Christ remains essential, not merely another or even a higher restatement of what has always been true from the beginning of the universe. For "this disposition of heart is *universally introduced and effected* through a unique historical event or, better, through a number of such events whose center is *Christ*" (#30). Thus Drey acknowledged a legitimacy, even a necessity for the "comparative religions" perspective for Christian theology without embracing the "natural religion" of the Enlightenment.

But the truly theological way of treating the historical phenomenon of Christianity is "as the center of all historical religious phenomena." And it was precisely this perspective which Kant seemed to have rendered impossible. For history can be known only from data, from what has been seen and heard and reported or recorded. It is a prime instance of *a posteriori* knowledge. It is reconstructed from sense data. It is, to use Drey's own word, a "phenomenon." But religious truth must be noumenal knowledge, which cannot be attained from phenomenal experience. That was why Kant had insisted that God could not be known but enters philosophy as a postulate of practical reason. The existence of God, like human freedom and immortality, must be posited in order to make ethics intelligible. Religion, when examined within the limits of reason alone, was seen to be the embodied support for ethical life. Christ became the exemplar or the archetype of the truly good life, the great example of the good person. But the archetype is found, not in history, but in reason alone. Theology, then, if it has any existence at all, must be an outgrowth of ethics, for only in the exploration of practical reason does one come by indirection to the realm of the noumenal. As Kant had demonstrated in establishing the limits of pure reason, no movement from phenomena to noumena, from sense experience to the "thing in itself," was possible. The attempt to treat Christian theology scientifically on the basis of historical phenomena was, then, absurd. Although Kant certainly cannot be described simply as a typical Enlightenment thinker, his religious thought does end by treating historical Christianity as one, even if the highest, exemplification of the truth which is available to all people at all times through the critical use of their practical reason.

Thus Drey's insistence on the historicity of Christian revelation was a position which could, at first glance, seem naive after the Kantian critical philosophy. But he did so by making historicity *intrinsic* to the truths of faith. Revelation does not only occur in history, history is an inner element of revelation. Any attempt to understand religious truth apart from its history is a misunderstanding, for the truth of religion is history. Franz Schupp has written that from Drey's placing of history within the truths of faith come not only the basic program of his attempt to establish theology as a science but that of the whole Catholic Tübingen school.[17]

Since historical theology is the necessary foundation for the other branches of theology, and Drey wrote that within historical theology Christianity must be studied "in a purely historical fashion" (#107), the methods of historical study are crucial for theology. Those methods are first and foremost the careful and intelligent reading of texts, i.e., the fundamental methods of history are hermeneutical. It is here that Drey's *Brief Introduction to the Study of Theology* agrees with Friedrich Schleiermacher's *Brief Outline on the Study of Theology*.[18]

Schleiermacher's attempt at theological encyclopedia had appeared in its first edition in 1811, eight years before Drey's. He had treated theology as divided into three divisions, each of which embraced several disciplines: philosophical, historical, and practical theology. Philosophical theology corresponds to what Drey named "foundational studies," the preliminary to the "specialized science" of theology (what we might call dogmatic theology). Both Schleiermacher's philosophical theology and Drey's foundational studies consist of apologetics and polemics. For both Schleiermacher and Drey theology culminates in practical theology, which is concerned with training leaders for the church. And for both, historical theology employing hermeneutical skills is central to the whole theological enterprise. Indeed, Schleiermacher wrote in the 1811 edition of the *Brief Outline* that "historical theology is the actual corpus of the whole of theological study and in its own way contains within it both other parts."[19] This historical theology is concerned with three issues especially, knowledge of Christianity in its origins, in its subsequent course of development, and in its current state.[20] Thus what Drey names "specialized science" or dogmatics is for Schleiermacher part of historical theology in that it is the study of the current state of Christian belief. Schleiermacher dealt with hermeneutics when treating of the knowledge of Christian origins, i.e., biblical and especially New Testament exegesis. But he noted that the hermeneutical procedures employed in New Testament exegesis are specific modifications of the general rules of hermeneutics.[21] Since knowledge of the later history of Christianity and of its situation in the present is dependent on the correct understanding of texts, what is said about the importance of hermeneutics for understanding Christianity at its beginning holds true for understanding Christianity at any time, including the present.

Unfortunately, Schleiermacher and Drey agreed, the general principles of hermeneutics were largely undeveloped in the decade when they were writing their theological encyclopedias. This deprives theology of the clarity which it should possess as a science, for the exegete and historian will find themselves being led by "some odd and unclear feeling"[22] in their interpretations rather than by rigorous hermeneutical rules. No one of their generation tried more energetically to establish hermeneutics on a scientific basis than Schleiermacher. In the year that Drey's *Brief Introduction* appeared, Schleiermacher was lecturing in Berlin on hermeneutics, although his lectures were not published until 1838, four years after his death.[23] The incomplete state of hermeneutics was, both Drey and Schleiermacher thought, one of the great problems under which the Christian theologian labored in their day.

But while Drey agreed with his great Protestant contemporary in Berlin on the centrality of history for the understanding of Christianity and therefore of the importance of hermeneutics, the deep structure of the *Brief Introduction* is very different from the *Brief Outline*. That difference is rooted in Drey's insistence, announced in the title of his encyclopedia, that theology must be treated as *Wissenschaft*, "science."

For most English-speaking people today, "science" means a method and the results obtained by it. The scientific method is that of hypothesis, observation (sometimes by means of a contrived experiment), and careful recording of the findings. The cumulative results of this method applied again and again are what is meant by scientific truth. For the

German-speaking world of the nineteenth-century, *Wissenschaft*, "science," meant a body of knowledge organized according to clear rules which related everything to certain fundamental principles and demonstrated how this body of knowledge was related to knowledge in general. This is what Drey meant when he spoke of theology as a science. And it was this which he thought Schleiermacher had failed to do rigorously enough. For Schleiermacher had defined theology at the outset of his encyclopedia as "a positive science whose various parts are only bound together into a whole through a common reference to a particular religion, which is for Christian theology Christianity."[24] In the 1830 edition he explained that by "a positive science" he meant a "collection of scientific elements which have no intrinsic connection as though they formed a portion of the organized whole of sciences necessitated by the idea of science, but only to the extent that they are required for the performance of a practical task."[25] But Drey insisted that this was insufficient. In his Foreword he affirmed that preeminent importance must be given to not presenting a science as though it were an accidental collection of operations. What, he wondered, would draw a student to the study of theology "if he has not grasped how the subject is related to his own innermost being, how knowledge of it is identical in its origin with the human spirit, how it derives from the human spirit and is established autonomously as an independent science, as a particular but necessary function of all human knowledge?" (p. 3). This was what Schleiermacher's encyclopedia could not provide a student, for if theology is a "practical science," it is by definition not "a particular but necessary function of all human knowledge."

If theology is a science at all, its constructive principle must be derived from the general theory of science which is provided by philosophy (#308). For Drey, that general theory had been set forth brilliantly by Schelling, whose *Lectures on the Method of Academic Studies*[26] he praised as containing comments "well worthy of attention, on a more scientific understanding of Christianity and a more scientific treatment of theology" (#84). What Drey took from Schelling in this regard was especially the understanding of science as an organic system. He informed the reader that his encyclopedia is organized in accord with "the nature of a positive science." A positive science for Drey is one whose content is given by history. But historical study, which is essentially hermeneutical, is a necessary but insufficient way of treating such a science. It must be organized in accord with "its essential similarity to a real organism" (p. 4). To study a positive science such as theology one must first recognize "the particular relationship of all sciences one to another, especially of the general to the positive." This is the result of "the organic nature of all human knowledge," i.e., "any body of knowledge is organized so that one science must precede another, that one must serve as the means of the other, and that the latter is utterly impossible without the former" (#86). No one part of an organism can be understood apart from the other parts which it serves and which serve it; to grasp the meaning of the part one must grasp the meaning of the whole. On the other hand, one cannot understand the whole apart from an examination of the parts. Theology is both a "whole" which has its constitutive parts, the subdisciplines, and is itself a part of a larger whole, human knowledge. So Drey was convinced that an encyclopedia could not be a mere recitation of the various branches of theology; the nature of theology, its origin and purpose, must first be presented to the student before the student could possibly grasp the rationale of its branches. And he was also convinced that theology could not be understood without showing how and why it emerges from the deepest ground of human existence as a necessary undertaking of the human mind.

Science is organic because it is rigorously organized knowledge, and human knowledge is organic. And human knowledge is organic because reality is organic. The particular cannot be understood outside the whole nor the whole apart from the particular. This is what Drey meant when, taking over a term from Schelling, he wrote that his goal in the *Brief Introduction* was the "rigorous scientific construction of theological study in general" and "the construction of Catholic theology in particular" (p. 5). "Construction," according to Schelling, is a holding together of the universal and the particular, the whole and the part, so that both become genuinely knowable. "Reality in general and the reality of knowledge in particular does not come either from the universal concept or from particularity. . . . The representation of the universal and the particular in their unity is generally called construction, which is not really different from demonstration."[27] Drey described the theological task as "the construction of faith through knowledge" (#45), i.e., the recasting of faith into systematic terms. And a system is understood to mean the laying out of the organic connections between the various images, concepts, doctrines, practices, and institutions of Christianity in such a way that they can be scientifically constructed or demonstrated, i.e., so that the generating and governing idea of Christianity can be seen in each particular image, concept, doctrine, etc., and each particular is seen as realizing in a unique fashion that general idea.

The Influence of Schelling

Schelling's understanding of science carried forward by means of construction is fundamental to Drey's *Brief Introduction*, but that does not mean that Drey can simply be regarded as a Catholicized Schelling. One might compare his use of Schelling to Thomas Aquinas's use of Aristotle: Drey took over fundamental attitudes and categories from Schelling but often used them in ways with which the philosopher would certainly have disagreed and created from them a new and distinctively *theological* system.

Certainly Drey applauded Schelling's fundamental contention about the study of theology: "What is essential in the study of theology is the combination of the speculative and the historical construction of Christianity and its principal doctrines."[28] Drey's discussion of theology in general and Christian theology in particular (##38–56) could almost be read as a commentary on this claim. Theology is the conceptual translation of experience according to Drey, and this translation "is partially traceable from the general laws of [the mind's] development and is partially made apparent in history" (#39). This is especially true of Christian theology since Christianity is rooted in specific historical claims. Yet this positive rootedness, this givenness of Christianity does not in any way exclude a genuine science [*Wissenschaft*] through the construction of ideas; the existence of natural science as a science demonstrated that, Drey thought. Nor did the "transcendent quality of its subject matter" make a scientific Christian theology impossible; this, he noted, was proved "by the example of philosophy," specifically Schelling's (#56). Schelling had written that he found it difficult to speak of theology's place among academic studies because he was forced to regard its distinctive form of knowledge and proper method as "lost and forgotten."[29] Drey agreed that the "confused and hesitant state" of theology, so prejudicial to Christianity, could no longer be tolerated; both "the spirit of our age" and the development of Christianity itself demanded "a rigorously scientific construction of theology."

> The spirit of our age is strongly scientific; an arbitrary and merely casual division and association of ideas no longer satisfy it, nor does historical proof by testimony to events. In all fields, it seeks the highest unity of ideas in construction. Only in this way does theology deserve to join the ranks of other positive sciences and assume the place which is assigned it as a scientific discipline both by ancient custom and by philosophy. (#56)

Schelling had pointed the way, no doubt. He taught that theology is "the highest synthesis of philosophical and historical knowledge," the point at which speculative philosophy became objective.[30] But Drey pointedly acknowledges Schelling's understanding of Christianity as *one* aspect of Christianity or as Christianity understood from *one* perspective. In 1800, three years before his *Lectures on the Method of Academic Studies*, Schelling had described universal history as falling into three great periods, that of Fate, Nature and Providence.[31] Initially the ruling power of the universe is experienced as brute force, an all-powerful but blind Fate. Then that power is recast as impersonal Nature operating by its own intrinsic laws. In the third period of history, however, what had been experienced as destiny or nature becomes known as Providence, the working out of the ideal in the real. Initially, Schelling maintained that the third period was yet to dawn and that no one could predict when it would begin.[32] Three years later, however, he wrote that the period of Providence, "the conscious reconciliation which replaces both unconscious identity with Nature and hostility toward Fate and sublates them into a higher stage of unity," had begun with the appearance of Christianity.[33] Drey echoes this claim when he describes Christianity as

> the period in our history when human beings, having been educated by God in numerous ways and having learned their true situation before God within the universe, recognize God's perfect dominion over them and the nothingness of all their egoistic self-willed efforts attempting, in their fragmentedness, to create their own world independent of divine influence and in opposition to it. (#29)

Drey's description of the human being as "saved from endless warfare with himself and with the world and from the consequences of that warfare and . . . accepted with fatherly love by God, to whom as a child he again draws near," parallels Schelling's reconciliation with Fate and

Nature by subsuming them in Providence. But Drey pointedly notes that this is "the philosophical meaning of Christianity" (#29). But this philosophical interpretation of Christianity tended to dissolve Christianity into one, even if the highest, instance of a truth which is exhaustively formulated by philosophical construction. Theology and, indeed, Christianity in general become symbolic images of what can finally be adequately stated only by philosophy. There are other ways in which Christianity must be viewed, other "meanings" which philosophy cannot exhaust.

One such other "meaning" is the historical. Schelling described Christianity as the culmination of a revelation which is co-terminous with creation. Drey could agree with that—in a sense. Revelation "has been from the beginning, continues in the present, and can never come to an end" (#16). The universe, i.e., man and nature, is the "unique" revelation, "absolutely complete and absolutely significant" (#17). The Spirit of God breathes through many forms, and both pre- and non-Christian religions can be genuinely revelatory of God (##25–27). Thus individuals and particular communities have had mediated to them God's self-revelation through the religious forms of their time and place and culture. "But this disposition of heart is *universally introduced and effected* through a unique historical event or, better, through a number of such events whose center is *Christ*" (#30). Christianity, therefore, both introduces something truly new into the world and is unsurpassable, i.e., not to be superseded by some subsequent revelation of God. That, Drey notes, is the historical meaning of Christianity, and it is an important point of difference between him and Schelling. For however much Schelling insisted that Christianity is truly historical, he tended to dissolve the "once for all and forever" aspect of the Incarnation. He dismissed the "empirical" interpretation of the Incarnation, "that God assumed human nature at a particular moment in time," as "absolutely unthinkable, since God is eternally outside of all time." "God's becoming human is a becoming human from all eternity."[34] Accordingly, Schelling had no difficulty in envisioning a revelation which would surpass Christianity, at least in any historically recognizable form.[35]

But Christianity apart from its historical form is not Christianity, Drey insisted. Christianity can only exist as "a particular religious institution with a definite character, interiorly expressed in a unique system of religious doctrines and externally expressed in a uniquely organized outward form—or church—for the purpose of preserving those religious doctrines and maintaining religious life as true and pure worship of God" (#31). This, Drey wrote, is "the theological meaning of Christianity," and like its "historical meaning," it cannot adequately be replaced by philosophy.

To give that theological meaning scientific form it is necessary to show how all Christian doctrines and the many aspects of Christian life are in fact generated from and contributory to one fundamental idea. And what is that idea which permeates every aspect of Christian life and thought and finds expression in all of them? The Kingdom of God. This is the original revelation of God which is one with the universe's existence (#27). It is *the* idea of Christianity, which has been obscured by the folly of humanity's attempt to assert its being over against God, which finds its highest expression in the closely allied Christian doctrine of the Incarnation, and which has been made concrete in human history by Christ, who thus became the visible head of the Kingdom. And its present tangible manifestation is the church (#32). Theology is, then, not only a matter of personal enrichment for those of a "scientific" or systematic cast of mind. The true end of theology is the furtherance of the fundamental ideas of Christianity in the church (#53). The theologian is in service to the church.

This is the final reason why Drey, however much he learned from Schelling, fundamentally disagreed with him on key issues. Schelling was an idealist philosopher who embodied the sovereign but lonely intellect confronting the task of speculatively uniting the many and the one, the real and the ideal; Drey was a theologian, which, he insisted, means a man of the church. It is not enough to achieve speculative knowledge of the ideas of Christianity; that is not what entitles one to call oneself a Christian. Nor is faith alone sufficient; it gives one "at best half a title," Drey wrote. "Only a way of being and acting" gives one full title (#36). Theology is in service of communal life.

A New Role for the Theologian

Here, precisely as a theologian, Drey is much closer to Schleiermacher than to Schelling. Schleiermacher had written in his encyclopedia that one who combined the theoretical and practical interests to the highest degree and in the greatest possible balance deserved the title "prince of the church."³⁶ Throughout his encyclopedia Drey maintained that theology is both theoretical and practical of its very nature, i.e., not merely a theory which is capable of being put into practice subsequently, but a theory whose practical import is intrinsic to its truth (#52). Like Schleiermacher, he gives theologians a necessary public role in the church. To be sure, theology contributes to the enrichment of the religious life of the theologian, but the theologian has an obligation to his or her community at large. Theologians must "contribute through the pursuit of their science to the realization of Christianity's ideas in the church" (#53). This is quite different from the description of the theologian's role which had been generally accepted in Catholicism for centuries. The theologian is no longer simply the one who explores the church's doctrinal pronouncements in order to elucidate them and defend them from misunderstanding or attack. That role had been essentially conservative; the theologian preserves doctrine and communicates it to future generations in the church. The theologian looks back to a tradition which it is his or her job to protect and preserve. Drey's description of the theologian's role is progressive; the theologian is charged with developing the tradition beyond its current state so that it can meet new questions, needs, and circumstances. The theologian looks forward to situations which the church has not met previously and seeks to realize the core ideas of Christianity in new ways. Obviously notions of tradition as *traditio* (the living process of handing on what has been realized to the future) and not *tradita* (finished positions to be handed on unchanged) and of development of doctrine and polity lie behind this. And certainly Drey and his colleagues at Tübingen were major figures in the emergence of a modern Catholic theology of tradition and theories of doctrinal development. But what Drey also did was to give his students and readers a new vision of the theologian's role in the church.³⁷

In this new role the theologian is kept orthodox by devotion to science. (It is noteworthy that Drey did not refer to the church's hierarchy as exercising this normative function for theologians.) Drey defined orthodoxy as "the effort to hold fast to what has been definitively closed in doctrine and to construe what is mutable in the sense of and in agreement with what has been closed" (#260). This is contrasted with heterodoxy—"the attempt to make what has been fixed mutable or to construe what is mutable in opposition to what is fixed"—and "hyperorthodoxy"—the denial of "the mutability of doctrine either because [one] rejects the idea altogether or elevates opinion into dogma." The theologian can avoid both of these extremes if he or she remains firm in the "scientific" (*wissenschaftlich*) viewpoint as expounded by Schelling and seeks the real in the ideal and the ideal in the real. "This strictly scientific construction" will enable the theologian "to maintain the middle path between two parties which now stand resolutely in mutual opposition, between the *immobilists* (*les immobiles*) who always cling to whatever is antiquated and discarded by the Spirit and the *eccentrics* who manufacture for themselves innovations quite independently of the Spirit and want to exchange whatever is most ancient for whatever is most recent" (#321*).

Drey was one of the first Roman Catholic theologians to recognize that the notions of doctrinal, liturgical, and institutional development entailed a shift in the theologian's role. The theologian could no longer be the defender of what has been taught and done. By virtue of ability, training, and leisure for study and reflection, he or she was charged with trying to discern what ought to be taught and done in new circumstances. The hierarchy could not be expected to fill this role; by and large, they lacked the requisite training and opportunity to engage the intellectual world of their time because of the burdens of institutional management. But this put theologians in the problematic role in which they so often find themselves today: maintaining the balance between "immobilism" and "eccentricity." In a sense, to use an American image, the theologian is in the position of a scout for a wagon train who must stay out in front of the wagons in order to explore what trails are safe, what dangers must be avoided, what paths lead only to dead ends, but who must at the same time never be so far ahead that he loses touch with the wagon train whose progress he serves. Few today will judge sufficient Drey's confidence in "scientific" method as a safeguard against imbalance. But many theologians will recognize their self-understanding in his call to serve the church by helping "to realize Christianity's ideas." "And this alone can be regarded as the true *end* of theologians and their studies as given both in the object of the science and in its presuppositions" (#53).

Michael J. Himes
Department of Theology
Boston College

Notes

1. Gerald A. McCool, *Catholic Theology in the Nineteenth Century: The Quest for a Unitary Method* (New York: Seabury Press, 1977), p. 265: "Of the theological systems which were represented in the nineteenth century debate over theological method, two are still alive. The two survivors are Kleutgen's neo-Thomism and Drey's Tübingen theology. Both are active participants in the contemporary debate over theological method."

2. Thomas Franklin O'Meara, *Romantic Idealism and Roman Catholicism: Schelling and the Theologians* (Notre Dame: University of Notre Dame Press, 1982).

3. For example, Edmond Vermeil, *Jean-Adam Möhler et l'école catholique de Tubingue (1815-1840). Étude sur la théologie romantique en Wurtemberg et les origines germaniques du modernisme* (Paris: Librairie Armand Colin, 1913).

4. Drey, *Kurze Einleitung . . .*, (Tübingen: Heinrich Laupp, 1819); the only other edition is a photographic reproduction of the 1819 printing edited and introduced by Franz Schupp (Darmstadt: Wissenschaftliche Buchgesellschaft, 1971).

5. When he was decorated by Wilhelm I of Württemberg in 1823, he received the honorific noble prefix and became von Drey.

6. "Revision des gegenwärtigen Zustandes der Theologie," *Archiv für die Pastoralkonferenzen des Bistums Konstanz* 1 (1812): 3–26; reprinted in J. R. Geiselmann, ed., *Geist des Christentums und des Katholizismus. Ausgewählte Schriften katholischer Theologie im Zeitalter des deutschen Idealismus und der Romantik* (Mainz: R. Oldenbourg, 1940), pp. 85–97; English translation by Joseph Fitzer in Joseph Fitzer, ed., *Romance and the Rock: Nineteenth-Century Catholics on Faith and Reason* (Minneapolis: Fortress Press, 1989), pp. 62–73.

7. J. S. Drey, *Dissertatio historico-theologica originem et vicissitudinem exomologeseos in ecclesia catholica ex documentis ecclesiasticis illustrans* (Ellwangen, 1815).

8. From Drey's *Tagebücher*, his notebooks, quoted in Geiselmann, *Geist des Christentums und des Katholizismus*, p. 183.

9. Drey's opinions about church governance and ecclesiology underwent change, however, after 1823 when his former student J. A. Möhler joined the faculty at Tübingen. Möhler's historical scholarship, especially in patristic theology, and his concentration on ecclesiological questions profoundly shaped the agenda of the Catholic Tübingen school and affected the outlook of his colleagues, Drey included. Gradually Drey moved toward a less Josephinist or Febronian view of church polity.

10. J. S. Drey, *Die Apologetik als wissenschaftliche Nachweisung der Göttlichkeit des Christentums in seiner Erscheinung* (Mainz: 1837–1847). The first

volume appeared in 1837, with a second edition in 1844; the second volume was published in 1842, with a second edition in 1847; the third volume appeared in 1847.

11. An excellent annotated bibliography of Drey's work, both published and in manuscript, has been given by Wolfgang Ruf, *Johann Sebastian von Dreys System der Theologie als Begründung der Moraltheologie*, Studien zur Theologie und Geistesgeschichte des Neunzehnten Jahrhunderts, Bd. 7 (Göttingen: Vandenhoeck und Ruprecht, 1974), pp. 20–54.

12. These notes are contained in three volumes entitled *Praelectiones dogmaticae* in the Wilhelmsstift Library in Tübingen. The fullest discussion of these in English, including numerous translated excerpts, is by Wayne L. Fehr, *The Birth of the Catholic Tübingen School: The Dogmatics of Johann Sebastian Drey*, American Academy of Religion Academy Series 37 (Chico, Calif.: Scholars Press, 1981).

13. *Geschichte des katholischen Dogmensystems. 1. Band. Geschichte der drei ersten Jahrhunderte oder erste Periode*. These have since been published in J. R. Geiselmann, ed., *Geist des Christentums und des Katholizismus*, pp. 235–331. The manuscript is in the Wilhelmsstift library.

14. In four volumes in the Wilhelmsstift library, listed as volumes 2, 3, 4, and 5 from the years 1812 to 1817, Drey's years of teaching at Ellwangen; selections have been published in Geiselmann, ed., *Geist des Christentums und des Katholizismus*, pp. 99–192.

15. Franz Anton Staudenmaier (1800–1856) taught at the Wilhelmsstift in Tübingen (1828–1830), Giessen (1830–1837), and Freiburg (1837–1855). Like Drey, he wrote on revelation and dogmatics and produced a major critical response to Hegel. During his later years he became deeply involved in political questions.

Johannes Evangelist Kuhn (1806–1887) taught at Giessen (1832–1837) and at Tübingen (1837–1882), where in 1839 he took over the chair of dogmatics from Drey. Like Staudenmaier, he became very involved in politics before and after the stormy year of 1848. He was a major opponent of neoscholasticism in the 1860s and 70s.

Karl Joseph Hefele (1809–1893), after teaching church history at Tübingen (1836–1869), became bishop of Rottenburg in 1869 and was a leader of the opponents of the definition of papal infallibility at Vatican I, although he later accepted the doctrine. His most influential work is his multi-volume history of the ecumenical councils.

Johann Adam Möhler (1796–1838), Drey's most famous student and later colleague, taught canon law and later church history at Tübingen (1823–1836) and then briefly at Munich. His two best-known works are *Die Einheit in der Kirche* and *Symbolik*.

16. Matthew Tindal, *Christianity as Old as the Creation, or The Gospel a Republication of the Religion of Nature* (London, 1730).

17. Franz Schupp, "Der Problem der Theologie als Wissenschaft: Eine Einleitung," prefaced to Johann Sebastian Drey, *Kurze Einleitung in das Studium der Theologie*, p. vi*. This is Schupp's preface to the photographic reproduction of Drey's book.

18. Friedrich Schleiermacher, *Kurze Darstellung des theologischen Studiums zum Behuf einleitender Vorlesungen*, ed. by Heinrich Scholz (Hildesheim: Georg Olms Verlagsbuchhandlung, 1977); this is the critical text of the second edition of 1830, which also contains in its notes the text of the first edition wherever it has been changed in the second edition. There is a fine English translation of the second edition by Terrence N. Tice, *Brief Outline on the Study of Theology* (Richmond, Va.: John Knox Press, 1966). No English translation is available of the 1811 edition.

19. *Kurze Darstellung*, 1st ed., p. 9, #36; Scholz, ed., p. 12, n. 1.

20. *Kurze Darstellung*, 1st ed., p. 28, #19; Scholz, ed., p. 36, n. 2.

21. *Kurze Darstellung*, 1st ed., p. 40, #30; Scholz, ed., p. 54f., n. 3.

22. *Kurze Darstellung*, 1st ed., p. 39, #27; Scholz, ed., p. 53, n. 2; Drey quotes this phrase from Schleiermacher when dealing with hermeneutics in #170.

23. Friedrich Schleiermacher, *Sämmtliche Werke*, Part 1, vol. 7: *Hermeneutik und Kritik mit besonderer Beziehung auf das Neue Testament*, ed. Friedrich Lücke (Berlin, 1838); critical edition by Heinz Kimmerle, *F. D. E. Schleiermacher, Hermeneutik: Nach den Handschriften* (Heidelberg: Carl Winter–Universitätsverlag, 1959). The English translation of the critical edition is *Hermeneutics: The Handwritten Manuscripts by F. D. E. Schleiermacher*, trans. James Duke and Jack Forstmann, American Academy of Religion Texts and Translations 1 (Missoula, Mont.: Scholars Press, 1977).

24. *Kurze Darstellung*, 1st ed., p. 1, #1; Scholz, ed., p. 1, n. 1.

25. *Kurze Darstellung*, 2nd ed., Scholz, ed., p. 1, #1.

26. F. W. J. Schelling, *Vorlesungen über die Methode des akademischen Studiums* (Tübingen, 1803); ed. Otto Weiss with further notes by Walter E. Ehrhardt (Hamburg: Felix Meiner Verlag, 1974). There is a nineteenth-century English translation by E. S. Morgan, *On University Studies*, ed. Norbert Guterman (Athens, Ohio: Ohio University Press, 1966).

27. Schelling, *Vorlesungen über die Methode des akademischen Studiums*, p. 46.

28. Schelling, *Vorlesungen über die Methode des akademischen Studiums*, p. 98.

29. Schelling, *Vorlesungen über die Methode des akademischen Studiums*, p. 90.

30. Schelling, *Vorlesungen über die Methode des akademischen Studiums*, p. 80.

31. F. W. J. Schelling, *System des transzendentalen Idealismus* (Tübingen, 1800); ed. Ruth-Eva Schulz with an introduction by Walter Schulz (Hamburg: Felix Meiner Verlag, 1957), pp. 272–273. This has been translated into English by Peter Heath, *System of Transcendental Idealism (1800)*, with an introduction by Michael Vater (Charlottesville: University Press of Virginia, 1978).

32. Schelling, *System des transzendentalen Idealismus*, p. 273.

33. Schelling, *Vorlesungen über die Methode des akademischen Studiums*, p. 84.

34. Schelling, *Vorlesungen über die Methode des akademischen Studiums*, pp. 91–92.

35. Schelling, *Vorlesungen über die Methode des akademischen Studiums*, pp. 98–99.

36. *Kurze Darstellung*, 1st ed., p. 3, #9; Scholz, ed., p. 4, n. 1.

37. Drey's part in the emergence of a new romantic-heroic role for the theologian and his similarity to Schleiermacher in this regard have been explored by John E. Thiel, "Theological Responsibility: Beyond the Classical Paradigm," *Theological Studies* 47, no. 4 (December 1986): 573–598.

Brief Introduction
to the Study of Theology

*with Reference to the Scientific Standpoint
and the Catholic System*

JOHANN SEBASTIAN DREY

FOREWORD

In writing a textbook on encyclopedia one can begin from one of several standpoints and aim at one of several purposes, and indeed, the standpoint and the purpose will determine the arrangement of the book.

Apart from the need which anyone feels who sets out to introduce others into some special field of knowledge, namely, to give people a sense of direction based on his insights into that field, the first task which the author must address is to give his audience an overview of the whole field of the science in its external boundaries and internal divisions set out as a blueprint; to note briefly what has been done in the field to this point, how and by whom; to inform them of the present circumstances of the science combined with rules for its study; and finally to equip them with some indications of the best books in the field's various branches. This is how most theological encyclopedias of an earlier time were written and how some of the most recent still are, among which I cite Planck's work[1] by way of example.

Someone else may prefer to consider the field of knowledge as an organic whole in which particular areas are gradually understood and interpreted in the spirit of the whole and the whole according to the natural interconnections of its parts. Such a person pays more attention to formal questions, allows the principal divisions of the science to develop out of this general perspective, establishes their interrelatedness, demonstrates their reference to the science's positive basis, and so estimates the greater or lesser degree to which an individual has to plunge into one or another aspect of the field of knowledge in order to meet his practical needs. Schleiermacher's *Brief Outline*[2] is designed in this way.

It seems preeminently important to me not to set forth a science, especially the science of religion, on the basis of what is simply accidental. Nothing is more generally discreditable to rigorous scientific thinking than when, in the first introduction to a science, it is presented to the eyes of beginners as matter of contingency, as something merely given, something which happens to be the case and about which consequently an equally contingent way of speaking has grown up, like a dead leaf on which travelers tread without knowing whence the wind has blown it. There is nothing more embarrassing to the interest which ought to draw the beginner to his field of study and which should be even stronger in this case because of the intrinsic importance of the subject, i.e., religion, than precisely this merely accidental style of presentation. How can a new student be filled with an inner spontaneous reverence for the subject of his studies, with a vital and awestruck zeal for it, if he has not grasped how the subject is related to his own innermost being, how knowledge of it is identical in its origin with the human spirit, how it derives from the human spirit and is established autonomously as an independent science, as a particular but necessary function of all human knowledge?

And so in the first part of this book I have submitted the fundamental concepts of the Christian theology—religion, revelation, Christianity, theology—to a thoroughgoing deduction and incidentally corrected some erroneous notions about them. Accordingly, the importance of the science for human beings and its necessity in the circle of the sciences, even in its present situation, are made very much more apparent and so become very much more interesting. But a rigorous grounding of all religious knowledge, which is possible only through a genuine philosophy of religion, lay beyond the purposes of this book, which were primarily to provide me with a textbook for lectures on encyclopedia in a course which I taught semiannually.[3]

In the second part—the actual presentation of the encyclopedia—I have chosen that way of dividing the theological discipline which seems to me to follow from the nature of a positive science whose content is empirically or historically given, and precisely knowable only because so given, but the presentation and explanation of which must rely on a more than merely historical construction if they are to be properly scientific. Because of its essential similarity to a real organism, such a science at last becomes truly organic in the course of its practical application.

In the explanation of the particular divisions of the science and its special disciplines I think it most useful to relate to one another an encyclopedia's two principal concerns, the formal and the material. Each division of theological study is therefore further subdivided into its disciplines in terms of how they provide fundamental concepts, of how they exhibit various relationships to other divisions and to the whole field of study, of the subject matter of each discipline, and of the methods of study employed in the particular divisions. As to the principles by which the special disciplines are constructed, although I firmly believe that they do not properly belong in an encyclopedia, I have nevertheless permitted myself an exception to the rule now and again, especially in cases when mistaken or false notions about these principles have been prevalent until now. I have also allowed myself in the notes to take positions on a number of issues or to call attention to various points, good or ill, about ways of thinking and acting in our own day. If these digressions seem less than an *opus supererogatorium*, I would respond that everyone writes from his own day and for his own day, especially in works on method.

I depart from the custom of those who begin an encyclopedia with a brief history of a field of study and of its literature because I think that the study of a science should conclude with its history, not begin with it. If the literature is treated as a something over and done with which is useful only at the outset, then the mind is simply filled with a long list of names and titles when attention could be much more profitably engaged on the preliminary and fundamental concepts of the science. In fact, the encyclopedia's purposes would be attained equally well if not better by the teacher's inserting the literature on a particular question at the appropriate place and appending the historical overview of the discipline at the end of his course of lectures.

It was necessary for me to say something about the internal organization of this book at the outset. Beyond that, I will not disguise the fact that concern for rigorous scientific construction of theological study in general, concern for the construction of Catholic theology in particular, and finally concern that up till now there has not been a wealth of encyclopedic treatments addressing the first two concerns, were the reasons for its publication.

Tübingen, July 4, 1819   Dr. J. S. Drey

PART ONE

General Introduction

Section One
Religion—Revelation—Christianity

I. Religion

#1

All faith and all knowledge rests on the dimly felt or clearly perceived presupposition that every existing finite reality has not only emerged from an eternal and absolute ground but that its temporal being and life remain rooted in that ground and dependent upon it. History shows that all faith and knowledge have proceeded from that presupposition, and philosophy makes at least demonstrable that, apart from that presupposition, there can be no certitude.

#2

Through this presupposition we are forced to acknowledge—or, better, we find immediately given—definite relations which finite realities must have to their ultimate ground and apart from which they are simply inconceivable. And further, these relations refer not only to the existence of these realities but also to the manner of their existence, to their nature and essence. They are only because and insofar as this absolute ground is, and they are and can become only that which this ground makes them to be, that which they are empowered by it to actualize—empowered under certain definite conditions. Within these conditions, they exercise this power of actualization according to definite laws and in a definite way which is the form of their life. As a consequence, they are related not only to their ultimate ground but to one another.

#3

Reflection, which is able to stand outside this nexus of relations and regard it as its object, perceives in it a universal *connectedness* and true *dependence* of all things in and to this ultimate ground: a connectedness in and of itself through having a common point of intersection, a dependence on and to that environment in which the individual comes into being and develops. Because of this connectedness within the whole and dependence within the individual the totality of things becomes a unity in multiplicity, i.e., a *universe.*

#4

This connectedness and dependence must be disclosed in real life, and all life's forms and manifestations can only express the dependence of each individual reality in its effects and action on the surrounding circumstances and a common orientation, the common directedness of all existents to the ultimate ground which holds them together as their center. Thus if the highest view of the world and its phenomena is that which sees it as a universe, so too the highest, truest, and most important study of particular things is that which observes and apprehends them in their relation to the universe.

#5

What then can be said about the particular with its life and activity in this view? On that level of being on which neither consciousness nor the freedom which accompanies it has emerged, dependence of the particular on its surrounding circumstances acts as simple natural law which is obeyed with unalterable necessity. In a similar fashion and with similar necessity, whether the circle is wide or narrow, attraction to a common center acts as a universal magnetic force. Thus, on the level of nature, the universe is perfectly obvious, clear and distinct.

#6

In an active being endowed with consciousness, the *experience* of connectedness and dependence is not separable from consciousness. It does not only come to consciousness but it arises with it—indeed, since a reality's whole being and nature is marked from its origin by that connection and dependence, the experience of that connection and dependence is one with original consciousness; in fact, it is this consciousness itself. This experience and its accompanying feeling are *religion.* Since religion is the first appearance of spirit in man, the original revelation of God to him, man becomes conscious of God as he becomes conscious of himself.

#7

Because the connection of things among themselves and with God is originally posited together with the idea of a world, and as this is prior to thought and before any feeling or consciousness which can occur in a reality regarded as simply existing, religion is consequently something truly *objective*. (This is objective religion in the fullest sense.) Because a person becomes conscious of this, because he feels and acknowledges this, it is *subjective*. But however much religious feelings and concepts shaped by human cultural conditions may differ among themselves, however much humanity may err in their interpretation, there always remains that objective foundation so that the appearance of religion in the human spirit can never be dismissed as a deception. It remains constant and unchanging, and humanity's errant affections may plot their course by it.

Note. The familiar question whether the term *religio* is derived from *religando* or *relegendo* may perhaps best be answered in light of the distinction advanced here. It seems to me that the answer is from both: through what is called objective religion man is bound; in feeling and reflection on himself and his interior life he *discovers* that he is bound. *Relegendo sentit se religatum.*

#8

Thus religion does not come to man from without (for, in fact, nothing whatsoever comes to him from without). It arises in him as the first feeling, his spirit's primal and essential orientation. It is not acquired subsequently through instruction or education nor initially self-generated in reflection. Reason, when it begins to perceive anything, first of all perceives God, then through him itself and everything else. But, like every other feeling, perception, conscious act, etc., religion too needs to be broadened and clarified in its concept and object. And to this end, instruction and reflection and assistance from within and without are useful.

#9

When religion is first manifested in a person, it appears as an impulse, an orientation, a way of acting, i.e., as something immediately practical in contrast to a purely theoretical product of the understanding. It can never shed this original and essential characteristic. And so in necessary agreement with the laws of the human spirit, like all other human impulses, it strives to transform itself into concepts and ideas, i.e., into clear representation. But neither any one representation of religion nor all such representations taken together, to the degree that they are simply representations, can be adequate to religion properly speaking; they ought to be referred to as *religious concepts*, a *religious system*. For two thousand years linguistic custom has tended to treat these terms as equivalent. But in every age zealous defenders of the essential character of religion have denounced this confusion of terms, which easily leads to conceptual confusion. And in our time, when the practical is so readily dissolved into concepts and systems, a careful distinction between them is required more than ever.

#10

The form in which the religious impulse, or if one prefers, the religious restlessness of the human heart, is expressed is usually that in which we recognize the relation of all things to God, but with this difference, that what in the latter case is regarded objectively as an accomplished fact, is seen subjectively as something one must bring to pass. That dependence on a higher reality (the eternal power) which is revealed in the existence of earthly things, the human being senses in himself as a drive toward and a demand for free obedience. That dependence on a universal order and interaction of all individual existents within the eternal mind is seen in the human being as a drive toward harmonious participation in that ordered whole. And the universal attraction of nature is seen in humanity as the force of love toward that eternal reality which has first poured itself into all things. Thanks to this similarity between the eternal laws of nature and the religious sense in human beings, nature too reveals religion, and *whatever is in accord with nature and not marked by self-will is a religious affection*.

#11

And as nature necessarily follows its course but with no feeling of force or necessity, religious affection responds gladly and willingly to the force of love for God. It feels its necessity but not as coercion and necessity, not as a force exerted on it from without, but as a conscious act which could not be otherwise. This is how the religious impulse operates wherever it is found in its pure form.

Note. A reappearance of this purity and of the congruence of religious phenomena within the human being with corresponding religious phenomena in nature is seen in that period of existence when the human person is closest to his original relationship with nature—in childhood. The child experiences the purest feeling for, the purest dependence upon and attachment to the ground of its being, its family, the circle of which is its world; this is religious feeling in its loftiest tone. This coincidence of the feeling for God, of whom the child has only an inkling and whom it can only envision in familial terms, with the feeling for the family itself may well be the reason that the ancients called two concepts, to our thinking quite distinct, by the same words: ευσεβειος, *pietas*. Other similar phenomena can only be mentioned here: the child's innocent devotion to nature, its love, hope, confidence, openness to people, the premonition of an unknown infinite power with which youth later fashions an ideal world in opposition to reality's leaden weight, the sense in all the dreams of youth that it is grounded in something deserving of love, the tenderness of its moral conscience, etc.

#12

The religious impulse is at work under these forms and must be at work in them if it is to maintain its original direction. But in the same act by which a person masters his ego and his egoism the possibility also appears for him to move past, if not objectively then subjectively, those ways of relating which we have discussed to this point. When this drive, which to this point has been described in its action and by the very terminology we have used almost as a kind of instinct, is raised in the person's self-consciousness to a free act of will, then it gives and receives direction from itself. It can now reflect upon its immediately obvious orientation, which is *fixed* in the will and is to that extent instinctual, and act upon it with self-determination. But by a defect (whose explanation is not necessary here) it can also be exerted as self-will in opposition to the will of God as manifested in the structure of the universe. And while this renegade will may be controlled by the power of the imagination drawing it toward the good and by physical forces, in its intention and action it has adopted an orientation contrary to its own primal nature. The will can do this, and experience teaches that it does do this.

#13

Where the final separation of freedom from necessity (which, in the religious emotions of childhood, acts *like* but not *as* natural necessity) is accomplished, man's internal and external life assumes a wholly altered form whose general characteristic is perpetual estrangement. With the same insistence that self-will attempts to transform *its* world into *the universe*, the will of God which rules the universe opposes this self-will and imposes on it as *peremptory law* what previously moved the heart as gentle spontaneous attraction. This imposition of law is the *conscience*, whose compulsion (categorical and explicit) precedes all action and, if an act is not in accord with the law, pursues the completed act in the guise of wrath and vengeance. This is the estrangement internal to man.

#14

Humanity deals with nature in a similar fashion. For self-will, when it elects itself as sovereign and acts as though it were, attempts to subject nature to itself and use it as a means to its own ends. But with fixed necessity nature serves and can only serve the will of God alone which is manifested in it and so thwarts self-will in all its attempts to act against God's will. Nature not only presents obvious obstacles in the way of self-will which it must surmount but also corrects it unobserved; for when to all appearances it is serving self-will, nature destroys it and its works with the same fixed necessity. This is the natural frustration of the godless which the Bible so often proclaims.

#15

But such estrangement is precisely contrary to the end of the whole order of reality; it is contrary to the eternal and absolute will of God; it is contrary to the condition of the free person manifested in the conscience. It can therefore only be regarded as something passing which stands in need of healing. Since we necessarily acknowledge that it must originate with God, this healing can not be looked for in the natural course of events. For conscience only *condemns* and nature only endlessly *negates* this dualism; neither frees man from it. We must anticipate a higher order of reality, an order which casts light on this estrangement in a way beyond nature as it now appears to man. This order of reality is what is usually termed *revelation*.

II. Revelation

#16

God's revelation is the expression of God's being in another which is not God and so to that extent outside God's self. Outside God's self is the universe and that alone. All God's revelation can thus occur only in the universe, and the universe is nothing other than that revelation. We divide the universe into two realms: humanity and nature. Through and in them God reveals God's self. The existence of things—including human beings—and their unchanging relationships to one another and to God are the content; the forms in which that existence is manifested, the forms and laws in and according to which those relationships unfold in the world's course, are the form of revelation. As with religion, revelation has been from the beginning, continues in the present, and can never come to an end.

#17

In this respect the universe is also the *unique* revelation, i.e., there is nothing which can be revealed by God to man save in man or in nature, and there is nothing which is without relevance to his or its relation to God. And so because the universe is the only possible revelation, it is also *absolutely complete and absolutely significant* revelation.

#18

It is so both with respect to God, who reveals his existence in the universe, and with respect to the perspective from which man—or any conscious being—views the universe *purely as revelation*, purely as God's own work. It ceases to be so, however, once humanity has moved past this original perspective to the second marked by self-consciousness and freedom (##7–12).

#19

For when a person adopts this latter standpoint (and everyone does so), the whole of God's revelation collapses into the hands and the will of humanity, becomes the work of humanity. The human being, originally the work of God, *exalts himself* as a free and independent being. The inner movement and impulse, originally God's power and Spirit, is now his own individual will which he determines for this or against that as it pleases him. All ideas now become his thoughts, which he fashions for himself. Even that clearest voice of revelation, conscience in the human breast, is the law which he gives to himself. The work which was divine in origin becomes the human being's own work by which he demonstrates that he is his own lord.

#20

So, too, with God's revelation in nature. In the same act in which man casts himself as "I," he also casts the external world, with respect to himself, as "Not-I," and in itself, as another "I" existing in itself, working of its own accord, and following its own laws, albeit unconsciously, and which he therefore hopes to bring under his power, if not wholly, at least in part.

#21

To the same degree as the feeling and consciousness of his own independence and belief in the independence of nature advance in the human person, God and his revelation recede into the background. God hides himself from the person who rejects him and henceforth reveals himself as the one who forgives the human being. Faith in this revelation is no longer given through immediate feeling or through immediate intuition but only mediated by reflection, hence lifelessly and ineffectively. The secular view of the universe is in the ascendant and undermines religion.

#22

And so a revelation is required which humanity can never attribute to its own power, which it can in no way explain as its own or nature's work, which it must acknowledge precisely as the immediate revelation of God, and of which, in the case of deliberate unbelief, it can deny the fact but not the character. In this revelation God will have to reveal himself to humanity as transcendent to its intellectual faculty and its consciousness, transcendent as well to its will and its moral faculties, and reveal himself to nature as mightier than it, as its lord and master. Only in this form can revelation require humanity to discern God in it. Only in this form can it drive the human being to recognize the original revelation which he allows to have force only when he chooses. Only in this form can it interpret that original revelation which he understands in whatever sense he desires.

#23

God has prepared the capacity and opportunity for this second kind of revelation within original revelation in that he has put under human control only the latter's effects—its facticity, so to speak—but never its genesis. The creative Spirit, as the intellectual breath blown into the universe, is now truly present in every intellectual act but remains truly the breath of God alone. And why could the original breath not be repeated in a second exhalation? As nature comes into being through the original creativity of God, why could this creative act not be renewed within human beings?

#24

Thus we grasp the significance of supernatural revelation and its true connection to natural revelation. Both being God's action, the former is nothing other than the latter. The operation of both is likewise the same: grant the intellectual act of the Spirit, and phenomena of the second kind of revelation spring into being as had the phenomena of the first kind. Spirit pours out from Spirit, here and there engendering what has been thought as in the beginning; the creative power forms and changes here and there as from the beginning. That this happens over and over again, that such events continue over the course of ages—is this unnatural or rather supernatural? Supernatural, of course, in light of what humanity in its folly makes of itself and nature around it, but entirely natural in light of what humanity and nature always were and ever remain before God and in the eyes of faith. For this reason, a miracle is given as a sign only to non-believers; to believers everything becomes natural.

#25

Reports of extraordinary events of this sort are found among all peoples. Their most ancient traditions begin with theophanies; these continue until a point in a people's history when heavenly forms recede before the flowering of earthly culture, the clear exercise of understanding. But they continuously manifest their existence and activity, their power and their will, in miracle and prophecy, in inspiration and the raising up of extraordinary persons whom they consecrate as their trusted servants and organs.

#26

With regard to the contrast between extraordinary revelations and natural revelation, we note that the further back in the infancy of the world extraordinary revelations occur, the closer they seem to natural revelations until at the very beginning they actually coincide. Later they separate and draw apart. But to the measure that extraordinary revelations become less frequent they become more universal and embracing and gain an expanded range of faith and action. They seem, however, to have as their purpose to be instructions and reminders given to a race which has separated itself from God, always to point us back to the original and eternal conditions of things, and to prevent humanity's destruction amidst the folly of its selfishness.

#27

The most ancient tradition of special divine revelations, the most reliable as to its historical credibility, the most fruitful in the purity of its concepts and their pertinence to religion, and so the one most commended by the strength of its warrants, is that which is found in the Jewish sacred scriptures. Beginning from the time when humanity in its infancy, instinctively following the prompting of religion, envisioned God and the universe as one and the former as within the latter, this historical account leads us through the period of awakened freedom, through the first signs of the negativity of self-conceit, and through the at first unrestrained, hence crude and often bloody eruptions of overweening selfishness; and so we come to the point when persons separate from one another, the primal family disintegrates into a multitude of different families and these again splinter into tribes, so that all are isolated; then the weak who are unable to stand on their own amid this general fragmentation and the now open war of all against each choose, from fear and for security, to attach themselves to the strong or are forced to do so by them. Once all human life begins to be marked by national differences in this fashion, naturally religion and revelation become so too. And we see this too in the sacred books of the Jews. Now God seems to be concerned only with this nation; they are depicted as the chosen people and everyone else as the rejected. But God's constant and powerful plan runs through all this special care and revelation and continually develops. Its range and perspective broaden continuously, and what mysterious prophecy had proclaimed in the beginning to this nation's ancestor becomes clear: God's directions and revelations were indeed entrusted to this nation but were not intended for it alone; in their further unfolding they are to embrace all nations and in their fuller light to establish one great community of all peoples and all nations under the rule of God. The world was such a Kingdom of God from its beginnings; the most primitive original revelation announced this Kingdom to mankind. But as humanity, ignoring the Kingdom of God, exalted itself *above* this original revelation, the revelation too was raised above humanity and so the Kingdom of God was assigned to a higher order of reality as mystery. —This is the historical course of revelation up to Christ.

#28

Its characteristic mark seems to be its historicity, as we have demonstrated in #22. Greater than humanity, more powerful than nature—this is what resounds from all the miraculous events of that history and from the no less miraculous course of that people's destiny in contrast to crudely sensual, egoistic humanity and all other nations. And in full accord with natural revelation, which in proclaiming the unchanging, eternal conditions of all reality to the roots of self-will which oppose them, condemns in conscience that self-will even as nature negates its effectiveness, we find curses and blessings pronounced throughout the whole of the law of Moses and the prophets which directly link good or evil consequences to an act and execute judgment through the nemesis omnipresent in all of history. Shortsighted critics have raised objection to what is precisely the most essential, the most sublime element in this revelation and divine pedagogy: "All human faculties are bound to what is earthly; not the slightest perspective beyond this life is opened; no immortality, no loftier reward is promised." But this misses the fact that this is precisely how the whole supersensual realm is introduced into the sensual world and brought into its immediate purview and empirical experience; it misses the fact that this is how all false theoretical and practical denials of a higher order of things which is not a prey to human selfishness are overcome. Faith must be forced upon sensual hearts enslaved to the self-deceit of selfishness; only in this way can that happen. What possible use could such a heart have for a bridge made of bubbles to get from this world to that? —Let the blows of an ever-present nemesis weary it as it pursues a road contrary to its God. Let it be brought first to awareness and afterward to conversion; then the vision of its faith will be restored along with the principles of its behavior. Then will the supersensual world become the only real one and this present world become the merely apparent one. Then, too, will the division between these two worlds, a painful illusion during the time of their separation, be overcome and the original unity of thought and desire restored, but on a higher plane. This turning point in humanity's religious history under the guidance of revelation is designated *Christianity*.

III. CHRISTIANITY

#29

In continuity with previous revelations, then, and in accord with God's manner of dealing with us human beings, Christianity can be seen as the period in our history when human beings, having been educated by God in numerous ways and having learned their true situation before God within the universe, recognize God's perfect dominion over them and the nothingness of all their egoistic self-willed efforts attempting, in their fragmentedness, to create their own world independent of divine influence and in opposition to it. It is the moment when a person freely submits to divine direction, the period when, as a result, he is saved from endless warfare with himself and with the world and from the consequences of that warfare and is accepted with fatherly love by God, to whom as a child he again draws near, the moment when he celebrates universal redemption. —This is the philosophical meaning of Christianity.

#30

As regards particular individuals, in all ages many may have experienced the longing for such a redemption, their hearts may have sought and found this dispensation, and to that degree they anticipated in themselves the Christian age. But this disposition of heart is *universally introduced and effected* through a unique historical event or, better, through a number of such events whose center is *Christ*. This is the (ordinary) historical meaning of Christianity.

#31

Through this event an array of previously unknown religious experiences and ideas were introduced among human beings. An array of other experiences and ideas of this kind which had previously lain dormant were given clarity and vitality. Through this new event many other religious concepts and institutions which had long dominated were corrected or discarded as insufficient, ineffective, and erroneous, or were given a higher significance, a revitalized strength, a purer meaning. This is Christianity considered as a particular religious institution with a definite character, interiorly expressed in a unique system of religious doctrines and externally expressed in a uniquely organized outward form—or church—for the purpose of preserving those religious doctrines and maintaining religious life as true and pure worship of God. —This is the theological meaning of Christianity.

#32

The historical event and the religious institution which it has created as its channel proclaim and explain themselves as the *final revelation of God*, the center of which is Christ, as has been said; this has definite effects. Viewed as revelation, Christianity is the summary of all previous revelations because in Christ God has *most perfectly* revealed himself to humanity. The idea of the *incarnation of God* and the idea of the *God-man* are inseparable from this final revelation. —Considered both in its highest form and in its goal, revelation can have brought about nothing less than the restoration of the condition of original unity under the form of a freely willed and conscious union. And from this effect there *must* follow the idea of a *universal redemption*; thus the idea of a universal *mediator and redeemer* is both necessary and intrinsic to Christianity. —In and through this oneness the *idea of a Kingdom of God* is once again discovered, both theoretically and practically, the idea which was expressed in the universe at its beginning, which grounded our first religious feelings, and which was forgotten during egoism's long dominance. This now appears as Christianity's supreme idea, that to which all others lead and from which they proceed. And Christ, who brings about this universal recognition, is therefore the *visible head of the Kingdom*, just as its visible expression and tangible realization is the *church*.

#33

Thus the full range of Christianity's religious ideas may be summarized as follows. God, who has revealed himself to human beings at various times and in various ways and who has never at any time or place permitted himself to go without some witness, has in this final age appeared to us in his Son, the most perfect revelation of his nature, who has taught us in word and deed how we should reject the godlessness and vain trifles of the world, the tragic errors of the earlier ages of fragmentation, and live soberly, justly, and piously in this world, looking forward to the fulfillment of the blessed hope that some day the great God and our Lord Jesus Christ will appear in the fullness of his majesty to us whom he has through his gracious gift purified from all sin and consecrated to himself as his own beloved people who seek only good works. And to this end, with the fullness of the divine power which is in him, Christ has announced to us that we are all to call ourselves his brothers and God our Father, sharing in his divine nature, and to become with him heirs of eternal immortal life.

#34

These religious ideas—Christianity itself—are of a wholly *positive kind*. They presuppose a definite and already completed development and change of religious levels; they mark a definite stage for humanity in regard to religion and develop—and will in future develop—totally new insights into humanity's relation to God and his decrees. In all these respects they entail some historical foundation. But they are positive in an even stronger sense, in that the origin of these ideas is explained as the result of a special dispensation, the result of an immediate intervention by God in the course of religious evolution; thus, when a person accepts these ideas, this is not regarded as his own discovery of them but as the response to a proclamation made to him from above. Under this positive character these ideas were spread abroad, widely disseminated with clear marks of God's extraordinary cooperation, and became the dominant religion among all *civilized* nations. This positive character of Christianity must not be overlooked or given cursory attention by anyone who intends to offer a fully accurate and authentic account of it.

#35

Since they give definite expression to the relationship between humanity and God, these ideas yield clear consciousness of this relationship within the hearts where they have taken root. To the degree that they hold sway in the heart, they give a particular character, tone, and color to the general orientation of that heart toward God. —These ideas are and can be designated a *definite and specific religion*, more properly a definite and specific *form of religion*. Because they refer to Christ in so many ways (##32–34), they are and can be designated the *Christian religion*.

#36

As a definite and specific account and clarification of those eternal and unalterable relations which constitute the objective foundation of religion generally, like those relations themselves, these religious ideas have an objective character. One speaks of them as though they were objects, and to the degree that the sum of these ideas make up the Christian religion, they can be described as the Christian religion in its *objective meaning*. —Because they ground a particular consciousness of God, a particular insight into the nature of humanity, and the many relations between God and humanity, and because the human person finds in them his highest, truest, and surest purpose, they can be described as *Christian religious faith* in its *subjective sense*. Finally, because the heart, captivated by this highest and surest purpose, takes its direction from this source of instruction and with pure devotion and willing energy strives to realize these ideas in life and action for itself and others, there develops, still in the subjective sense, *practical religious devotion*, true religion of the heart (*religiosity*), that *living Christianity* which is the will of God and of Christ, the vocation and the mission of *the Christian*. To that name mere knowledge and speech about the ideas of Christianity lay no title, faith alone lays at best half a title, and only a way of being and acting lays full title.

#37

But notwithstanding this practical tendency of religion generally and the Christian religion especially, indeed in service of this practical tendency, there can be and is in fact a properly intellectual engagement with the ideas of religion and so, in our case, with the ideas of Christianity. Such an engagement, although ordered toward religion, is no longer termed religion on account of its properly theoretical nature (for, by contrast, the nature of religion is purely practical). It is named for the loftiest subject which it takes as its object of study: *theology—doctrine of God,* also *doctrine of religion, science of religion.*

Section Two
Theology—Specifically Christian Theology

[I. General Meaning of Theology]

#38

Theology, as a purely intellectual engagement with religion, arises necessarily within humanity, i.e., it arises in accord with the necessary laws of the total nature of the human person, specifically those according to which he seeks to clarify his experiences although they are in themselves obscure and to give them permanence although they are in themselves fleeting, so that he renders permanent in *concepts* what has affected his heart pleasantly or painfully and can by conceptual means deliberately recall and renew whenever he wants what first affected him as external and alien factors. As the human being deals with experience in general, so must he deal with religious experiences which preeminently concern him.

> *   The ancient but recently renewed argument about the part which the understanding, i.e., general intellectual faculties considered purely as such, plays and can take in religious matters would be very easily resolved if people would only be precise in expression and really wanted to understand. The discussion and resolution is found in ##9 and 36–38; we give further elucidation in what follows immediately.

#39

Thus theology is in the religious area what in every other area of human concern is termed apprehension, conceptualization, or knowledge. It is the expression and result of those mental laws by which our minds resolve all data, external and internal, all experiencing, feeling, and willing, into concepts. The process by which the mind does so is partially traceable from the general laws of its development and is partially made apparent in history. In this brief outline of the evolution of theology we will follow the same pattern we employed in the brief outline of religion and revelation.

#40

One's theology depends on one's religion, one's stance toward God; this is our first axiom. One's theology depends on one's level of spiritual culture; this is our second. One's theology changes, i.e., is formed, expanded, and supported, as one's stance toward God (discussed in the first section) and, along with this, one's spiritual or intellectual culture change.

#41

In the early stages of childhood religious experience has not yet broken through to reflection, and the interior world is not yet really distinguished from the external; a person lives more experientially than conceptually. Thus, at this stage, there can be no theology, only religion. But because even at this stage a person's natural desire drives him to center in some way his religious experiences and he is unable to do so conceptually, he does so through his powers of imagination and sense perception. And so he connects his experience in one case with a natural event, in another with a natural object (e.g., a spring, an altar stone). The spring and the stone, nature in general, become for him signs and reminders of God, who fires within him a longing for a still greater epiphany; thus the stone where the Holy gently touched him becomes sacred for him. This is mythic and symbolic consciousness, which in this period of childhood substitutes for theology. We find it in a truly pure and pious form only in the most ancient parts of the Bible and in a form compounded with conceptual understanding and gross sensuality in pagan mythology.

#42

With the passage of time this symbolism becomes history from which humanity, now become more capable of thought, abstracts its first religious concepts in order to appropriate them as such, independently of symbols and in themselves. This is the beginning of theology. It comes into existence in this way, and this is the only way it can come into existence. The influences on its formation are, first, the quality and purity of the symbolic system itself; second, what surrounds it and is connected with it within the broader history and native outlook of nations and regions; and third, natural aptitude for thought, for whatever affects the development of intellectual culture acts through human initiative and divine guidance.

#43

So it is on a foundation of historical traditions and with the assistance of various operations of the intellectual faculties that the religious ideas and concepts are built which either from the beginning or soon after are the common possession of many of an intellectual cast. *Religious theories* are devised, taught to others as *religious doctrines*, and spread from the few to the many. The religious ideas which they enshrine may be more or less pure, more or less developed, more or less coherent. We must expect differences; peoples' theologies can only be understood in terms of their histories.

#44

If in the many ways people interact with one another, different religious theories come into fundamental conflict with one another and so give rise to polemics, or if to a developing culture its myths and symbols no longer seem adequate or doubts arise about their historical authenticity and that of tradition generally, or if finally the complex of religious doctrines which worked before no longer meets spiritual needs, then a demand appears to sift religious ideas and theories and provide them with a firmer foundation. This is done by gradually shifting one's view from a simple collection of religious ideas to a system; in this way there gradually forms what we at our present stage of cultural development usually mean by the term *theology*. —Here we can see when and how theology gradually came to be from the story of biblical symbols and the complex of Mosaic religious notions, as in another case we know how and in what ways Greek mythology expanded into natural theology or religious philosophy.

#45

The general characteristic of this transformation or this new way of thinking which affects all religious concepts is that instead of the *immediate certitude of vision* there is *mediated certitude through reflection*; in place of simple *faith*, there is *knowledge*. And as through this transformation genuine theology first comes into being, so through it we arrive at the vocation and task of theology in the strict sense, which is nothing less than *the construction of religious faith through knowledge*.

#46

This construction can be done in two ways, just as knowledge itself, or assurance mediated through reflection, has two aspects. First, the religious notion (or the sum of such notions) may be traced back to an originating fact as something immediately certain, as the notion's probative authority. In this case, the construction is purely *historical* as is the corresponding knowledge and certitude. When elaborated into a theology dependent on faith in revelation, this mode of procedure is called *theological supernaturalism*. Or second, the notion may first be fashioned from historical tradition, including revelation, into an idea and so an immediate certitude is reintroduced by means of rational insight. In this case, the construction is *philosophical*, rightly termed scientific, as is the corresponding knowledge and certitude. This mode of procedure thoroughly carried out is called *theological (positive) rationalism*. So, supernaturalism is not knowledge about what had hitherto merely been objects of faith; it is simply knowledge of and about faith itself. By contrast, rationalism seeks knowledge of the objects of faith and hopes to transform faith into knowledge.

> * There are also two other ways to turn religious faith into knowledge. The first, which regards all merely historically based faith as dead and thus useless for awakening religious life in any way, seeks knowledge in immediate *vision* and certitude in *immediate inner experience* of what outwardly one speaker passes on to another as a dead word—even though God's word. This is the meaning and the aim of *mysticism*—practically considered, the flower of religious life, but theoretically viewed, a source of innumerable delusions and errors. Besides, this mode of procedure is so exclusively subjective that it is open neither to mediation nor to positive statement. —The second excludes any positive encounter and collaboration with God in the genesis of religion, explains religion as simply a work of human reason abstracted from itself and from nature, and rests all certitude in religion on the mediation of human reason alone. This is *naturalism*. It is obvious that

this is as exclusively subjective in itself and as distorting of any positive element as mysticism; it is also clear that it is not the same as rationalism, with which it is often confused due to the fact that scientific interest in religion currently alternates between rationalism and naturalism.

#47

The historical construction of religious belief can also be pursued in two ways, because of the different sources of historical tradition and different opinions regarding them. If scripture alone is accepted as the means of the tradition of the ideas of religious belief, then construction proceeds by way of scriptural interpretation; then the whole of theology is exegesis. But if there exists a living objective reality which is generally recognized as the continuance of the originating event and therefore as its most authentic tradition, then the historical witness is found in and through it. This reality is the church.

* Since scriptural interpretation, purely as such, is wholly and entirely open to subjectivism, the obviously contradictory situation arises that faith must be supernaturalistic and theology merely subjective and naturalistic. On the other hand, it is equally obvious that such theology can only be made *positive* and *effective* by a church.

II. CHRISTIAN THEOLOGY

#48

Following the general considerations about the origin, form, and concept of theology which we have seen to this point, it is now an easy matter to turn from them to Christian theology. Christianity is a particular positive religion (##34–35) with a distinctive set of religious ideas (##31–32) which, when absorbed into the human heart, establish there a religious faith (#36). In spite of its practical tendency, it not only permits a purely intellectual engagement with its central concerns but, following the necessary course which religious belief always takes, demands it to the point that construction of this faith through knowledge becomes a necessity, at least for some people (##37–45). This construction of the Christian faith, embracing the whole range of its concerns, is *Christian theology*.

#49

This construction is both more natural to Christianity than to other forms of religion and easier to do, because its religious ideas were initially proclaimed by its founder *in a pure form*, i.e., independent of symbols and myths, without any other concrete point of reference than his own person and history—a point of reference which it possesses because of its nature, because it is a positive religion, and because of the form in which it was publicly manifested to those for whom God first intended it.

#50

Christian religious belief spread and took root in the form in which Christianity first appeared, that is, in the form of a history. Because of what they saw, the first believers were convinced by what they heard. And the original vision was continued even after Christ's departure in the institution which represented him, and with this vision also the conviction and faith of Christians. Accordingly, there could not have been any question of theology in the sense discussed above. But both the historical foundation of Christian belief and individual doctrines of the Christian faith were called into question and disputed by opponents. The apologetic enterprise which necessarily resulted (cf. #44) produced the first attempts at a Christian theology which in form and direction corresponded exactly to our ideas, save that these attempts failed to grasp them systematically.

#51

Only later was a comprehensive theology attempted in a form and fashion which can not be evaluated here. It began and was elaborated under circumstances which we have described as the general causes of the development of theology (#44). It has long since become a specialized science in response to the needs of those who are driven to construct religious belief through knowledge by general cultural movements or their own speculative interest in the subject or the importance which religious faith has in their hearts. For such people this construction takes on a personal subjective necessity; the number of such individuals is not and never has been insignificant.

#52

But theology as a special kind of knowledge does not depend simply on a subjective and therefore free turn of mind which would render it accidental to certain individuals and to religion itself. It is a *positive* life's work, i.e., a *professional science*, both with regard to its *end* and the *method by which this can alone be accomplished*. Although a kind of knowledge, theology is *practical* even in itself, because one never in any case knows simply for the sake of knowing, and the object of theology, religion, is thoroughly and eminently practical. Christianity especially has proclaimed the realization of its ideas in human beings as the distinguishing mark of a new age of the world and regards itself not only the means of this realization but its organ and instrument, both of which are found in the *church*.

#53

Thus, those who engage in the science of the Christian religion with energy and success have not only the possibility of richer formation and continuing animation of their own religious sensibility, which is always the *fruit* of real theological studies for them, but also the obligation to contribute through the pursuit of their science to the realization of Christianity's ideas in the church. And this alone can be regarded as the true *end* of theologians and their studies as given both in the object of the science and in its presuppositions.

#54

The church, then, is the true basis of all theological knowledge. From it and through it the theologian receives the empirically given content of that knowledge. Through it must all his ideas attain reality, else they dissolve into airy, unsubstantiated speculation. In the church knowledge must again pass into practice, lest it remain idle, purposeless digression. The church is for the theologian what the state is for political science, what the animal organism is for medicine: the concrete expression of the science itself, that through which it becomes positive.

#55

Consequently, because churches differ from one another, each has its own theology. And the differences between theological systems is evidenced not only in variations in particular doctrinal statements but in the organization, foundation, division and development of the whole science. We are offering an outline of *Catholic theology*, and this entails the construction of Christian religious belief through knowledge based on the Catholic Church and in accord with its mind for the purpose of working with this knowledge in appropriate ways within that church toward Christianity's ultimate goal.

#56

Furthermore, the construction of Catholic theology, like all theological construction (#46), can be pursued in two distinct manners: in the purely historical fashion through reflection or in the scientific fashion through construction of ideas. We emphasize the latter because we regard it not only as one possibility but as a necessity. It is a possibility—because all the objections which have been lodged against the possibility of a science of Christianity are based either on the positive character of Christianity and its doctrines resulting from revelation or on the transcendent quality of its subject matter (see Planck's *Grundriss der theol. Encyclop.* ##29 and 170). But that the characteristic of givenness, of positiveness, does not exclude a science of that which is given we demonstrate by the example of natural science. And that the transcendent quality of its subject matter does not render such a form of knowledge impossible we prove by the example of philosophy. And it should go without saying that we claim no greater perfection for our science of religion than the aforementioned sciences have attained in the present stage of rational knowledge. We regard a rigorously scientific construction of theology as a necessity, given the spirit of our age and the current stage not only of theology but of Christianity itself. The spirit of our age is strongly scientific; an arbitrary and merely casual division and association of ideas no longer satisfies it, nor does historical proof by testimony to events. In all fields, it seeks the highest unity of ideas in construction. Only in this way does theology deserve to join the ranks of other positive sciences and assume the place which is assigned it as a scientific discipline both by ancient custom and by philosophy. —This science, which deals with the loftiest of all subjects, has for many years been in a confused and hesitant state which has had a very prejudicial effect in ways embarrassing to Christianity and its actualization. A half-educated empirical naturalism has denied revelation and positive Christianity. Supernaturalism has been able to respond to this only weakly and never really to refute it, since it stands in the same unhappy position as naturalism and so opposes to it no higher scientific principles and combats it with the same weapon—mere reflection. Between these two there has been a third contestant, one which has not untied the knot but hacked it through: mysticism, which renounces all science and intellectual study and hopes to attain the goal of religion without them. This confusion in the realm of the science of religion *can only* be resolved through a whole new foundation for the science on a level which rises above all the previous debates and from which alone the various contenders can be understood. From what has been said it can be decided whether or not there is real need to ascend to this level.

III. Scope, Content, and Organization of Theology

#57

As regards its scope, Christian theology includes everything which is the subject matter of Christian religious belief (#48). Its limits therefore can not be set only by what has to do with Christianity as a temporal phenomenon, that is, in its usual sense, but by the idea in which its whole religious vision is summed up. From this idea must be constructed the science of the Christian religion. We have already mentioned this idea (#32), and although this is not the place to give its complete deduction from the fundamental elements of Christianity, still the key points of this deduction may be noted.

#58

The original image of God in Jewish sacred scripture, on which the Christian scripture is dependent for the history of the divine work of teaching and for its whole preparation, is God the *creator*, and (for that reason) *Lord, ruler of heaven and earth*, not only in the moral sense in which everyone who has any knowledge of God regards him, but in a political sense which accords with the political mind of the ancient world. And so the nations of the earth are his vassals (Israel being the best beloved among them), and kings are his viceroys, for he alone is the true King, the King of kings. The strife of nations one against another, the manifold injustices committed by these viceroys, and the oppressive weight of oriental despotism gave birth to the idea of a new dispensation and the establishment of the Kingdom of God, in which all nations will be reconciled, where divine benevolence will establish justice and peace, where universal joy will reign, through a man of Israel's lineage, raised up by God and fashioned as a *worthy* regent. This man and his kingdom became the expectation of the Jews. —This idea, true in itself, was the result of the experience and suffering of that nation and rooted in the spirit of the ancient world; it was the highest religious idea which both suited the age and prepared the way for still higher visions in a future age when the earthly husk of an actual state could be sloughed off as a type so that a purer ideal image of the Kingdom of God might shine forth.

#59

This was accomplished through Christ. He refined the material idea of *an earthly Kingdom of God and worldly dominion* into the purity and universality of a *heavenly kingdom*, a moral kingdom within the universe; he transformed the king of a nation into the Father of humanity, and the viceroy of the king into the Son of the Father, the Firstborn; he gave the whole of past history on which the Jewish idea of the messiah depended, its intrinsic significance as well as its higher meaning in that he allowed it to be recognized as gradually unfolding stages of God's education of humanity, the moments and epochs of his Kingdom, the periods of humanity's tutelage, as it were; and with the moment of his own appearance he introduced the epoch when the mystery of the past would be uncovered and when from this brighter present a broader vision of the future could be seen. This is the idea of the Kingdom of God in the meaning which Christ has given it: God's decrees concerning human beings and the world, the eternal thought of his Spirit, revealed and realized in sacred history, but only gradually and so still hidden from human eyes, until in the fullness of time Christ appeared who now reveals those decrees, proclaims them in definitive form, and unites them in his own history.

#60

That this idea is Christianity's supreme idea (as it is the authentic idea of all religion; see ##1–7) is clear from the fact that no notion or doctrine, not even another idea within Christianity can be mentioned which is not included under this idea, ordered toward it, or derived from it. That it is also clearly the central idea of the New Testament is shown by the fact that every single doctrine and every practical precept of Christianity—all God's judgments and revelations, all God's acts in creation and history, all the promises of earlier and later ages, Christianity itself in all its dimensions insofar as it is one particular temporal event—are contained in it.

#61

Because it is historically based, Christian theology embraces both that historical period which secular history designates by the term "Christian," and the whole of world history from the beginning; it interprets this history for the science of religion according to the insights found in the teaching of Christ and the apostles. The specific treatment of what has been called Christian history in the narrow sense properly belongs to a special discipline within theology. Thus it is incorrect to say: *"Christian theology is the science of that religious theory which Christ introduced and should be kept confined to issues intrinsic to the history of Christ and his teaching."* —It is a necessary implication of the universalism of the Christian religion that it is linked historically and theoretically to the *pre-Christian* world. It is impossible to appreciate the breadth of its religious theory or plumb its depth without specific reference both to Old Testament history and doctrine and to historical developments and religious conditions among other nations.

#62

From this it may readily seem that we intend to extend the domain of Christian theology far beyond its usual limits. But this seeming pretentiousness is immediately justified by the demands of the idea of science; even in the eyes of those who do not rise to such lofty considerations, any pretentiousness will disappear if they will only recall that Christian theology has advanced its claim against limiting its scope hesitantly and under the insistence of the scientific mind-set. Any decent compendium of dogmatics can provide evidence of this. The only point of disagreement is that they may regard as an incidental claim and arbitrary addition what we correctly deem intrinsic to the nature of science. But we can not be concerned that someone may be unfamiliar with the demands of science. The vocation for rigorous science is not for everyone of every sort. It is only given to a few to embrace that vocation; it is both their delight and their calling to instruct others in fields where many can at best be only spectators.

#63

What constitutes the content of Christian theology is sufficiently indicated in the account of its general scope. This content is historically given in the faith of Christians; theology must ground it scientifically. In such an undertaking what must be done first and foremost is to show how historical knowledge (that something is and what something is) differs from knowledge about its foundation (that something is necessarily so and why something is necessarily so). As before, what the nature, form, and methods of science are must be assumed as known. Here only the most fundamental principles by which we determine divisions and procedures in the whole domain of the science can be noticed.

#64

Unquestionably the first principle is: the whole of Christianity as a given and positive reality—in history and doctrine—can be initially known only empirically and historically, and historical knowledge of it certainly must precede scientific knowledge, because the former is the material substance of the latter. It goes without saying, therefore, that there is a *historical theology*, and it embraces much more than is usually reckoned under this heading. All of theology can be historical, and it usually is so whenever the construction of Christianity from its ideas is regarded as impossible. Whatever is not apt for construction from ideas (and much that the theologian has to know is of this kind), whatever the theologian learns not in the form of science but as straightforward historical information or as the data of scholarship, is the proper subject of historical theology—or, better, belongs to the historical study of theology.

#65

The second principle is: empirical historical information about Christianity is elevated to the level of real science when its content is traced back to an idea and the idea is unpacked in a systematic deduction of the concrete particular. We have noted this idea in ##58–61. It was first posited and made known through Christianity. But it is grounded in reason, a true idea of reason, which, like all such ideas, was first energized thanks to the stimulating light of educative revelation so that it emerged independently in reason. Through the absolute necessity and truth which the idea of the Kingdom of God possesses in reason, all its manifestations in humanity's history, all the doctrines of Christianity which set forth and explain the mysteries within this history (the plan and organization of the Kingdom) attain the same character of necessity and truth. As Christ himself rendered the whole of history prior to his time clear in these ideas and his apostles did likewise, so scientific theology further renders Christ's history clearer in its ideas and brings these ideas together with the earlier ones into a unity. And did he himself not give the example for this continuing clarification? Did his apostles not do so even more obviously?

#66

From this the connection of these two principle branches of theology to one another becomes clear. It is not so much their material as their form of knowledge which distinguishes them. One and the same thing is first *grounded* by way of historical study and then *systematically shaped* by way of scientific construction. —Hence these two branches can never really be separated from one another, only distinguished. Historical knowledge, or rather its results, is present throughout the whole science. The branches are thus related to one another as the *historical propaedeutic* to the *science* itself.

#67

Any historical study has two components—that which one desires to study and possesses as knowledge once one has studied it, and the way one studies something and subsequently possesses it as knowledge. The first is the historical subject matter itself, the second the historical construction of the subject matter. This must also hold true in the historical propaedeutic to theology. *What* one intends to study in it so as to gain knowledge is precisely *historical Christianity* in its broadest dimensions; *that by which* one studies it is its *historical medium of transmission*, by which is understood here exclusively or at least primarily a written medium of transmission; *how* one studies and comes to knows historical Christianity from its documents is learned from the particular scholarly techniques and principles according to which the written sources are read and interpreted. This is what is understood by the term *exegesis*.

#68

The task of the historical propaedeutic is thus to set forth historical Christianity from (primarily) written documents through their careful reading and interpretation. The presentation of historical Christianity is the *end* and chief concern, the sources are the *medium*, and correct application of scholarly techniques and principles to those sources yields the *historical construction*. The role played by ideas in a truly scientific presentation of Christianity is played by historical sources in this case; what the scientific method does in the one, exegesis does in the other.

#69

As a temporal phenomenon, Christianity has a *beginning* and a *development* which grows out of its beginning. In the historical treatment of matters, these two can and must be distinguished for many reasons. Christianity in its beginning form is called *primitive Christianity* and, with reference to its written medium of transmission at this period, *biblical Christianity*. —Christianity in the form of its full development to the present is the *Christian church*. The study of historical Christianity—as the first principal division of the theological propaedeutic and its purpose—falls then into two major sections: the study of biblical Christianity (*biblical theology*) and the study of the history of the Christian church (*historical theology* as that title has usually been used).

#70

As historical studies, both depend on historical media of transmission, especially written sources, the first on the Bible, the second on ecclesiastical documents. With reference to this distinction between the Bible and ecclesiastical documents, the scholarly techniques which pertain to the study of history on the basis of its sources and the principles on which the interpretation of these sources depends may again be divided into two headings, *biblical exegesis* and *church historical exegesis*. The study of these two headings is thus the second major task of the theological propaedeutic, but because of the nature of the subject matter, since this study is the most immediate precondition for historical investigation of Christianity, it must precede the latter.

* Exegesis, which has been treated up until now by theologians as one particular discipline within the range of its studies, is a fully universal discipline in its own right and is required in all branches of human knowledge when there is any question of the interpretation of written sources. To the unique respect which the Bible as *sacred scripture* commands among Christians we undoubtedly owe those immense labors by which exegesis has been brought to that perfection and universal application which now allows its employment by non-theologians in their areas of study; there is no longer any need for many different disciplines in light of the peculiar qualities of various kinds of documents, but they can be treated as a number of species under one genus.

#71

Scientific theology takes the results of biblical-historical theology (#69) and by means of its own unique construction—by transforming historical material into ideas (#65)—builds it into a true system of Christian religious doctrine. Because it takes as its basis the controlling idea of Christianity, the Kingdom of God, it constructs this system in a twofold fashion in accord with the two perspectives in which that idea is presented in the Bible. The Kingdom of God has an *ideal aspect*, from which it is seen to be the inner core of all God's decrees in the universe, a pure inner core of the ideas which have been proclaimed by Christ and which, when organized by the science of religion, produces the *doctrines of the Christian religion*. And it has a *real aspect*, from which those decrees are seen as realized and those ideas are actualized and attain objectivity in definite tangible forms. During the stage of the Kingdom of God which Christianity has introduced, this objectivity in definite tangible forms is *the church*. From this point of view, the church is fundamental with regard both to its outward organization and to its inward elaboration of a scientific construction. Then the *theory of the Christian church* emerges as the second major division of the science along with Christian doctrine and is the latter's real and immediate foundation.

#72

A *general foundation of the science* should properly be distinguished from the study of the science within these two major divisions; indeed, this general foundation must precede the other two. For when theology, as a *positive and particular* science, requires to be derived from science in general, a demonstration is needed of the connection between its principles and those of reason which in their content and form are set forth in philosophy. Obviously the development of science insists that its idea and its guiding principles be *constructed beforehand*. And Christianity's unique position in relation to and in contrast with other similarly distinct forms of religion makes necessary both an *apologetic for the doctrines of the Christian religion* and, since the basic claim of a higher origin for these doctrines has been under attack for so long by naturalism, a *defense of that origin* on the other hand. All this is preparatory to the science and can only be done with the aid of principles which lie outside and, since it is a positive science, above it. Since these general principles can only be obtained by borrowing them from philosophy, the general foundation for the science can for that reason be called *the philosophy of the Christian religion*, or from its largely—indeed, if one wishes, exclusively—apologetic orientation, *apologetic theology* or *apologetics*.

> * The need for this foundation is already acknowledged in the Old Testament. At an earlier time, it was incorporated in an incomplete form in the so-called *prolegomena to dogmatics*—mistakenly, because it ought not to be the foundation for this special field alone but for the whole science. —Likewise, it has been too narrowly termed *general dogmatics* or, more correctly, *general theology*. It clearly does not belong among the exegetical disciplines, however; rather, it stands to scientific theology as exegesis does to historical theology.

#73

Thus all *the theologian's knowledge of Christianity* is contained in the historical propaedeutic (##66–71) and in the science itself (##71–73) but not his whole *study*. The use which he should make of his knowledge within the church (##52–54) makes necessary for him beyond this knowledge a *special introduction* to the *skills and methods* by which it ought to be used in the church and on it. The need for such an introduction, which is, of course, thoroughly practical, is probably obvious without any proof, but it may easily be demonstrated from the outward form taken by the influence of religious ideas on the church in accomplishing practical goals and their mode of procedure. In its outward form this influence appears as *church leadership, church government*; as regards its mode of procedure it is—like all government—

education, the religious education of humanity in and through the church. But government and education are skills, and special training and direction must precede the exercise of a skill.

#74

This direction or instruction is no longer theology proper, for it teaches nothing more about God and divine things. Instead, it is a technical training, a technical instruction for the scholar in divinity needed for the exercise of his science, which teaches him the forms and means by which, in accord with his vocation and the purpose of his studies, he can have an effect on and in the church. Thus this technical training belongs to his program of studies. When it has been called *applied or practical theology*, it has been improperly so called and "theology" is used in the extended sense to which the term can always be stretched. The full course of study for the theologian thus includes three major subjects or three major divisions: the study of historical propaedeutic; the study of the science itself; the study of practical technical training.

> * How well this manner of division of ours within theology functions compared to those in use until now, we leave to impartial judgment. On this question, compare the better-known textbooks of theological encyclopedia.

IV. Theological Encyclopedia

#75

To this point we have demonstrated that the subject of all theology, *religion*, is the earliest, most essential, most universal, and so highest phenomenon of the human spirit. Further, we have discussed the historical form of all religion in which we find it posited, *revelation*, as that religion's objectivity, a necessity from every point of view, and its authentic actualization, through which God's educative providence safeguards it against human arbitrariness and its concomitant dissolution into mere subjectivity. We have considered Christianity as a phenomenon which includes earlier religious phenomena and its significance with regard to those phenomena. And finally we have deduced from its subject matter that theology, including Christian theology, is a necessary expression of the human spirit. We have also led the beginning theologian to the only point from which he can enter upon his science with full appreciation, from which he will not stumble into it accidentally and blindly but can take it up with steady attentiveness. We have already discussed this in the Foreword.

#76

The basic notions which we have established thus far of Christian theology, its scope and its contents, as well as its divisions, provide also a preliminary view of the treatment of the science, of its significance and the interconnection of its parts. We see how and why the whole science is formed this way in the first place. Nevertheless, up until now the introduction is too general, and only the broadest major divisions of theological study have been mentioned. But this is still not enough to keep one from blindly fumbling about within the various branches, which is every bit as bad as blindly fumbling into the whole study, and to prevent rote learning, which is at best learning about externals. Thus for the lively understanding of a science in all its branches there must be preliminary to the study an outline which includes a division of the whole science into all its parts, which allows us to see the importance to the science of each part in turn and the way all of them are united into a single whole. This preliminary outline of the science is called *encyclopedic*.

#77

An acquaintance with all the branches which together make up the whole of the science in its various aspects is necessary for the beginner so that he can gain for himself a complete preliminary notion of it and know what he is setting out to do in the science as a whole. The encyclopedic outline thus divides each of the three major divisions of theological study (#74) into its subordinate parts.

#78

The derivation of these subordinate branches from the field at large must be done through a construction similar to that by which we derived the major divisions from the idea of the science. If the major divisions have been formed correctly through this construction, then in each of the subordinate branches will be found one of the *key ideas* of the larger division which is drawn from it and which determines the necessary *content* of that branch. When formulated as a clear idea, this content makes it easy to set out the *scope* of each subordinate branch and to determine the *fundamental perspective* from which one begins in each branch and the *guiding principles* which must be followed within it. In this way each part is formed by and imbued with the spirit of the whole.

#79

And so we see also the *connection of the subordinate branches*, their interaction with one another, the *value* which each branch has as an integral part of the whole, and the *relative necessity* of using each branch according to the kind of effect on the church which one can expect from it in time. —An introductory propaedeutic to all the subjects and issues raised up to now is both desirable and essential for the beginner in the science. And the theological encyclopedia provides the theologian this introduction .

#80

In addition to the *subject matter* which is dealt with in a science, attention must also be paid to the form. And if form can scarcely be deemed a casual concern even in less strict and organized fields of inquiry, in the strict sciences it pertains to the very essence and is of the utmost importance—both for one who teaches the science and for one who intends to study it. *The study of method* is therefore naturally and necessarily connected to the encyclopedic outline of a science. In fact, the one cannot be easily separated from the other; instead, they must be treated together, else one puts oneself in the uncomfortable position of having to deal with the science's formless matter on the one hand and contentless form on the other. Therefore, since we have already indicated in the foregoing sections the *forms* and *methods* in which an explanation or study of theology *in general* can be pursued, they will assume more definitive shape in each important branch of the science.

#81

As soon as one grasps the positive character of theology and so the necessity of including positive knowledge within it, one feels the need for this study of method or, better, the need for an initiation and introduction into the study of theology. But, of course, everyone does not present an introduction of this sort in precisely the same way, still less from the same point of view, as we do. The contemporary situation of the science and the demands arising from it determine the spirit and content of such introductions. —In the age of the initial reform of theology from those limitations imposed on it by the long dominance of Aristotelian scholasticism, the first task was to purge it of fruitless, pointless speculation, useless word games and logic-chopping and barbarous language, and to make the science more Christian and the theologian more reverent. Next there had to be insistence on the spirit of Christianity and its doctrines, their deeper grounding in the Word of God, and in general a more practical style of theologizing. Aside from the mystics, who as the natural opponents of degenerate speculation had attacked the abuses of scholasticism even before the reformers of the sixteenth-century (1), this was done from the Catholic side by Erasmus[4] (2) and from the Protestant side by Melanchthon[5] (3). Both of these men stressed the need for knowledge of languages in addition to broad scholarly and scientific education.

> (1) Among the people who almost a full century before the Reformation understood and stoutly proclaimed the need for an improvement in theology those especially deserving mention here are Chancellor Gerson[6] in his *epistola ad Studentes Navarrenses*; and Nicholas de Clemangis[7] in his *opus de Studio Theologiae*, which Lukas d'Achern[8] has incorporated in volume VII of his Spicilegium.
>
> (2) *Ratio sive methodus ad veram Theologiam perveniendi*, published in 1782 at Halle by Semler[9] and in a noteworthy edition in 1786 at Prague.
>
> (3) *Brevis discendae Theologiae ratio*, Opera, Tome III.

#82

Because the reformation of theology which was then under way made the science historical and strove constantly in this way to give it a more solid foundation, an ever greater need was felt for prior historical-exegetical studies. But both history and exegesis were insufficiently developed, and neither had yet been raised to the level of special theological disciplines. As a result, all these studies together with the relevant literature were gathered into collections under the heading of "introductions," "theological compendia," etc. —The best known and in many respects still the most valuable are by *Annat*[10] (1), *Possevin*[11] (2), *Mabillon*[12] (3), and *du Pin*[13] (4). Among older Protestant works of this kind special mention ought to be made of those by *Hyperius*[14] (5) and *Georg Callixtus*[15] (6), and among later works those by *Buddaeus*[16] (7), *Pfaff*[17] (8), and the elder *Walch*[18] (9).

(1) *Apparatus ad Theologiam positivam methodicus*, Paris, 1700, Tome VI, in quarto. Subsequently often republished.

(2) *Ant. Possevini S.J. Adparatus sacer ad Scriptores Veteris et Novi Testamenti, eorum interpretes, Synodos, Patres latinos et graecos, horum versiones, theologos scholasticos, quique contra haereticos egerunt, chronographos et historicos ecclesiasticos, eos qui casus conscientiae explicarunt, qui canonicum jus sunt interpretati, poetas sacros et libros pios, quocunque idiomate conscriptos—ordine alphabetico digestus*, Tomi II, Venice, 1603–1604, in folio.

(3) Joh. Mabillon, O.S.B., *Tractatus de studiis monasticis*, Paris, 1692. This had been published in French several years previously; the book's apologetic bias gives it a decided narrowness.

(4) Louis Elie du Pin, *Methode d'etudier la Theologie*, Paris, 1717; Latin translation by Christell in 1722 at Augsburg; revised French edition by Abbé Denonard, Paris, 1768.

(5) *Andr. Hyperii L. IV de Theologo, sive de ratione studii theologici*, Basel, 1572.

(6) *Georg. Calixti Adparatus theologicus*, Helmst, 1656.

(7) *Joh. Franc. Buddei Isagoge historico-theologica ad Theologiam universam, singulasque ejus partes*, Leipzig, 1730, in quarto.

(8) *Christ. Matth. Pfaffii Introductio in historiam Theol. literariam*, Tome III, Tübingen, 1724, in quarto.

(9) J. Georg Walch's *Introduction to the Theological Sciences*, Jena, 1753. —and *Bibliotheca theologica selecta*, Tomes I-IV, Jena, 1757–1765, large octavo.

Anyone desiring fuller information on literature of this sort in an earlier period will find it in Stephen Wiest's[19] *Introductio in historiam literariam Theologiae revelatae, potissimum catholicae*, Ingolstadt, 1794, and in the already mentioned work by Walch, *Bibliotecha* I, pp. 1–25.

#83

Once this newer theology had attained a more finished form and divided its material into clear major sciences and these in turn into subordinate categories, and once the need was felt for some scientific foundation for the historical thinking which dominated the whole scientific field, introductions to the study of the science had to be brought into line with these altered conditions. Much of the scholarly attention which had earlier been paid to these introductions was now devoted directly to the special branches of the science. Furthermore, in sorting out these branches technically, as well as in the general account of their subject matter, their limits, and their ends, it was now necessary to take special note of the form of the science and the connections and relations of its branches to one another as well as of the connection of theology to other sciences and scholarly fields. And lastly, there was need to decide on the best and most effective method for the whole study. The literature and history of theology in its branches was still taken over from the old introductions. The encyclopedias and methodologies of *Wiest*[20] (1), *Oberthür*[21] (2), and *Gmeiner*[22] (3) were written in this fashion; *Nösselt*[23] (4) and *Planck*[24] (5) have published more detailed introductions of this kind. *Herder's Letters*[25] (6) was written in another spirit and for a totally different purpose.

(1) *P. Stephani Wiest Specimen encyclopaediae ac methodologiae theologicae in usum academicum*, Ingolstadt, 1788, editio sec. mutata, octavo.

(2) *D. Franc. Oberthür in Acad. Würceb. S. S. Dogmatum Prof. encyclopaedia et methodologia theol.*, Salzburg, 1786, octavo.

(3) *Gmeiner Xaverii Schema encyclopaediae theologicae—per terras Austriacas*, Graecii, 1786, octavo.

(4) Joh. Aug. Nösselt, *Instruction for the Education of Beginning Theologians*, Halle, 1791, 3rd edition, 8; most recent edition, vol. 1, 1818, vols. 2 and 3, 1819.

(5) *Introduction to the Theological Sciences* by D. G. J. Planck, Leipzig, vol. I, 1794; vol. II, 1795, octavo. —*The Summary of the Theological Encyclopedia for Use in His Lectures* (Göttingen, 1813) by the same author is an abstract of the *Introduction* in which the outline and development remain the same but to which the author has appended his expanded and corrected views on particular points.

(6) *Joh. Gottfr. von Herder's Letters Concerning the Study of Theology in the Second Expanded Edition, 1785, Collected Works, On Religion and Theology*, vol. IX, Tübingen, 1808, vol. X, number I. —The author offers here in his own unique fashion extremely interesting suggestions and observations on the spirit and study of the Bible especially, but also on all

the more important points of the system of the Christian religion. An actual formal encyclopedia subsequently appears in volume X, number II: *Essay on How a Young Theologian Should Employ Three Academic Years*.

#84

In the last three decades, the great revolutions which have occurred in the realm of German philosophy have naturally affected theology too and in fact, because of the inner connection between the two sciences, have done so in some ways more strongly in theology than in the other sciences. As a result, the feeling has grown that there is need to reform the science itself as well the introduction to it in a way which more adequately responds to the requirements—now become very much more stringent—of a positive science. And since the whole spirit of modern philosophy has aimed at stronger grounding of issues in their deepest principles and with equal insistence at scientific form in their organization and systematization in their working out, those who have in recent times written introductions to the study of theology have adopted these same primary goals. Among the first attempts of this kind belong the encyclopedic presentations by *Thym*[26] (1), *Tittmann*[27] (2) and *Schmidt*[28] (3), which add to inflexible formalism the obscurity of critical philosophy. This is also in part the case with the textbook by the always very systematically organized *Dobmayer*[29] (4). Aimed at very specialized concerns and so somewhat limited as real handbooks of theological encyclopedia are the otherwise acceptable books by *Daub*[30] (5), *Schleiermacher*[31] (6), and *Thanner*[32] (7).

(1) Thym's *Theological Encyclopedia and Methodology*, Halle, 1797.

(2) J. A. H. Tittmann, *Encyclopedia of the Theological Sciences*, Leipzig, 1798.

(3) *Theological Encyclopedia for the Lectures of J. E. Chr. Schmidt*, Giessen, 1811, octavo.

(4) *Mariani Dobmayer Systema Theologiae catholicae*, Tome I: *Encyclopaedia et Methodologia*, Salzburg, 1807, large octavo.

(5) Daub, *Introduction to the Study of Christian Dogmatics from the Standpoint of Religion*, Heidelberg, 1810, large octavo.

(6) *Brief Outline of the Study of Theology for Use as Introductory Lectures Delivered by F. Schleiermacher*, Berlin, 1811, in octavo.

(7) *Dr. J. Thanner's Encyclopedic-methodological Introduction to the Academic Scientific Study of Positive Theology, Especially Catholic Theology,* Munich, 1809, octavo.

Particular remarks, well worthy of attention, on a more scientific understanding of Christianity and a more scientific treatment of theology are found in Schelling's *Lectures on the Method of Academic Study,* Tübingen, 1803, esp. in lectures VIII and IX.[33]

#85

And finally, inseparable from an introduction to the study of theology is a clear statement of the presuppositions of this study, i.e., a clear statement of all that one who devotes himself to this science is expected to bring to it because he cannot presume that he will acquire these skills in the course of his studies: inescapable preconditions from which he may not dispense himself if he wants to have a complete grasp of his science and which those who will teach him as professors of the science must require of him. This will receive special attention in the next section.

Section Three
Presuppositions of Theological Study

#86

The presuppositions of the study of a positive science or the preconditions for a successful commencement of such a study stem partly from the particular relationship of all sciences one to another, especially of the general to the positive, and partly from the particular relationship of the student to the science to which he intends to devote himself. The first relationship is the result of the organic nature of all human knowledge, in such a way that any body of knowledge is organized so that one science must precede another, that one must serve as the means of the other, and that the latter is utterly impossible without the former. The other relationship is the result of people's different subjective casts of mind and the relation of this way of thinking to the organic whole of knowledge, so that a person can only advance successfully in any particular line of knowledge in a way that corresponds with his particular cast of mind. In short: the presuppositions of theological study consist partly in certain preliminary studies and partly in certain aptitudes which one must bring to its study.

#87

Preliminary studies are either *general* or *special*, i.e., required for anyone seeking scientific education in any area or required by the theologian in his special sphere. Thus the former are general educational means, the latter necessary auxiliary studies geared to a definite purpose—theological science. By their nature, both can be either *simply scholarly* or *rigorously scientific* studies (preparatory studies and sciences; auxiliary studies and sciences).

#88

Among general educational means, and definitely among those which do not exist in scientific form, we encounter first the constituents of any humane education, so called because of its importance for humanity. Surely it is superfluous to give any demonstration at this point that the theologian—quite apart from the concerns of his science—must be a broadly and liberally educated person. But beyond their general affect on human sensibilities, the studies in question possess this special distinction: they are extremely well adapted to prepare one for scientific studies and moreover enrich one who studies them with an array of linguistic and other scholarly tools which he greatly needs as indispensable aids in his science. For happy and effective work in his science it is absolutely essential for him to have been so educated.

> * What Erasmus thought about the humanistic education of the theologian can be found in his book mentioned above,[34] pp. 22 ff.; on the relevance of this education to academic scientific education, see Schelling, *On the Method*, etc., Third Lecture.[35]

#89

Furthermore, some of these studies are included among those which are indispensable for the theologian in his own area. These are the studies of ancient languages, specifically those in which the primary sources of biblical and ecclesiastical Christianity were written. It is obvious that one must begin learning these languages at the start of theological studies; indeed, a certain level of proficiency in them must be reached, because anything to do with the mechanics of learning languages, which is a simple matter of memory, requires youth, fresh ability, and leisure time which a candidate in a strict science has usually already lost. The situation is quite different when we turn to advanced language studies which can be begun in one's maturity and which no one can ever claim to have studied enough.

#90

More or less the same holds true in *historical studies*. They too belong under general educational means, they too are necessary auxiliary studies for the scholar, in some respects more proximate and immediate than language studies. In addition, the theology of Christianity rests on a historical foundation, and because Christianity is itself history, a large and important part of world history, from a historical perspective it is neither comprehensible nor intelligible apart from its connection with world history. And so, when some background of historical knowledge is required for any work in the historical study of theology and when this background can and must be continually expanded by further study, it is certainly not demanding too much of a beginner in theology that he be expected to come equipped with a good idea of general history.

#91

As might be expected, among the historical knowledge which is especially needed by the theologian in his sphere are knowledge of the religious and ethical positions of peoples and nations of every age and, above all, knowledge of various religious ideas and systems. Among these latter, there are again some of particular interest for the Christian theologian partly in their own right, partly because of their influence and effects, and partly because of their impact on Christianity. To be specific, this includes especially the religious systems of the ancient world, preeminently those of the ancient eastern world, as well as ancient history generally, because the origin and primitive form of Christianity are intimately bound up with them. The more familiar one is with the ancient worldview, the clearer will the various parties in the confusion of earliest Christianity become for him. So whoever would most readily understand the full history of Christianity must provide himself with the widest and most complete overview of human history.

* We cannot treat here of those studies which serve as auxiliary studies to history itself.

#92

But no less important for the theologian than the fields mentioned to this point which are merely areas of scholarship are the preliminary studies which are of a more rigorously scientific character and which are grouped under the heading of *philosophical education*. Although there is general agreement on this, there are nevertheless various opinions on the specific connections which exist between philosophy and theology. Consequently some further comment on this point may be in order. The source of the differences in opinion lies in part in the confusions of form with essence and of the subjective forms of one age with the one objective fundamental form which is sought and, with greater or less clarity, found in them; and in part in mistaken notions, formed by oneself or inherited from others, about what philosophy is supposed to do for theology. We shall begin at the point on which there is greatest agreement and from there seek to understand the disagreements.

#93

On the whole, there is full agreement that philosophy is the formal study of human thinking and knowing, that philosophical education as a general scientific preparatory exercise in thinking is therefore necessary for the beginner in theology, and that it remains necessary at all times and places for the theologian. Since this is, in fact, the case and the reasons for it are accepted by everyone, it would be superfluous to say anything more about it.

#94

But philosophy has value for other sciences as more than simply tools and exercises. It possesses a still higher value for them as the science which is universal in both form and content and as the type and unifying center of all other sciences. —The very idea of science, the idea of individual and special sciences, the idea of their connection with one another, the idea that each of them is a necessary function of the thinking and inquiring mind—where does this come from if not philosophy? —And the very ideas which are the focal points of the positive sciences and whose full content are explored in those sciences, where else are their scientific quality, their elegance and their independence of time-bound and so imperfect realizations appreciated if not in philosophy? —Finally, where else would the mind seeking for scientific knowledge of all positive fields learn to see whatever is empirically and historically posited as necessary, to resolve it into its ideas and then deduce it from them, except in philosophy?

#95

If, therefore, an authentically scientific outline of theology is a real need both in and of itself and especially at the present time (#56), there is likewise need for philosophical education prior to this study and for philosophical thinking to continue to be used in subsequent theological work. Certainly it is true that the use of a particular way of philosophizing (a particular system) is inevitable. But when based on this an attack or an objection is raised against any use of philosophy in theology or against the use of a particular philosophical system in it, the objection can only come from those who do not recognize that one cannot philosophize at all without philosophizing in some particular way. They do not realize that those who pretend to dispense with every set form precisely by this fact adopt one particular form in their philosophizing. They do not know that from of old various philosophical systems have been used in doing theology and that theology has been assisted and advanced by every one of them. They do not see that when problems have appeared in theology because of this use of philosophy, these problems have never been as great and by their nature can never be as great as the problems which must ensue and have ensued from the lack of philosophy, whether due to ignorance or to unfounded pseudo-knowledge, rash contentiousness, and unrestrained, all-corrosive criticism.

#96

This is in no way to deny that, depending on the type and method of thinking about the task of philosophy and grounding it, one system may be more congenial to the spirit of Christianity and hence of greater usefulness to Christian theology than another. Unquestionably, that system has to be regarded as the best which, because it is already religious at its base, proposes the same view of history and the world, refuses to separate them from God but instead denounces belief in their autonomous existence as the worst of errors, and concedes to them only such reality as is consistent with regarding them as God's revelation unfolding in two perspectives or two fundamental and essential forms. While from the theoretical side this system is in entire agreement with the views of Christianity, from the practical side it assists the theologian to appreciate Christianity's moral imperative and proclaim it to others with living belief. That imperative is to see oneself as the worthy revelation of God (his image), and in order to do this, to recognize the eternal design for human self-development in the whole schema of divine revelations, especially the perfect revelation (Jesus, the God-man), and so come to authentic religious life, harmony with God through harmony with his revelations.

#97

But if, after all this, someone should still ask, "What can philosophy have to do with a *revealed* theology?" we reply—beyond what has already been stated in #56—that all revelation comes from God's eternal absolute reason and proceeds from that reason and so can not be totally alien to human reason in which the divine reason is preeminently revealed. Furthermore, we state that the whole purpose of revelation can only be humanity's education by God and that consequently in revelation's history and doctrines there must be a plan, order, and system which people of faith must discern and formulate clearly, indeed, that they absolutely cannot avoid doing so. And we further claim that even a true and authentic revelation's significant meaning is lost to science in the course of time unless the events and doctrines involved are reduced to immutable ideas of reason, thus eliminating their accidental quality, which can render their real source doubtful or unclear.

#98

There seems no need at this point to say anything more about the special connections which exist between certain philosophical and certain theological disciplines, since those connections are generally acknowledged and can be more easily taken up in the encyclopedic outline. It only needs to be noted here as a general rule that it is hard to think of any philosophical discipline, even one which has no direct relation to any branch of theology, whose study would be without value to the theologian.

#99

If the preliminary studies mentioned to this point come from the connections between the particular science of the theologian and the clear universal and objective demands of his kind of study, there are yet other more subjective requirements which are preconditions for this study stemming from the student's personal stance toward his science. And if the point of the former can be described as necessary *preparation*, the point of the latter is a no less necessary *vocation* for the science. Vocation or, what is the same thing, the inner natural aptitude for any undertaking whatsoever, consists in possessing the qualities needed for the undertaking to have any possibility of success. This is what is needed to undertake any scientific study: the vocation consists in those qualities without which one cannot transform a bunch of lifeless, externally derived ideas through free reconstruction into living knowledge nor actualize this knowledge in some sphere. Accordingly, anyone who possesses those qualities through which one can refashion the material of theology into living knowledge and use it fruitfully and effectively in practical work within the church (##52–54), is called to the study of this science.

#100

Among those qualities foremost, naturally, stands *intelligence*, or a certain array of intellectual abilities of a particular cast. For the scientific character requires the talent for historical and philosophical construction (##63–66). Grasping the enormous mass of historical data demands no ordinary memory. Discriminating among them, separating the true from the false, requires no ordinary understanding and acuity, no ordinary power of discrimination. And finally, the theologian's practical orientation requires quite exceptional skills in communication, teaching, and explanation. This much can be said in general. In any given case, however, each one's own work and experience must teach him the sufficiency or insufficiency of his intelligence, if he has no friend or counselor, or if he will not accept his friend's counsel.

#101

Along with these specifically intellectual gifts one also looks for other qualities of the heart which are therefore of a moral kind in the theologian. For the specific subject matter of theology is the Holy, and this is a matter more of the heart than of the head. —Among these gifts must first be mentioned a lively sense for the truth which dwells in the heart and guides and directs the head. Beyond the fact that truth is the goal of all knowledge and every science, the kind of truth which is sought in theology, namely, religious truth, has a value which surpasses all others and the greatest and most far-reaching effect on the character, virtue, life, and happiness both of individuals and of entire nations. No other truth has been sought with so much and so enormous effort of the human spirit, and no other has been so completely lost in the anxiety of the quest, indeed no other has been so often attacked and rejected. Thus, above all others it requires the most forthright, most careful, and most persistent seeker. And indeed, it can be said without the least exaggeration that it requires this kind of seeker now more than ever.

#102

In addition to desire for the truth, which is or at least ought to be the preeminent and universal possession of every scientific inquirer, because of his special science and his special calling the desire for the Holy, the religious sense, must be quickened and developed to the highest degree in the theologian. This must not be understood as merely the stage of religiosity or the mere capacity to be moved by religious truths and experiences. For this is present in any heart which has not yet been hardened, and so the vocation for theology would be universal. Also, this must not be understood as merely a further development of that stage or that capacity, which can be the result of the individual's spiritual orientation, his positive education, his fortunate state and outward circumstances, or of some nobler motive. For once again, such advanced development of the taste for piety has always been found in many people, and so the vocation for theology would still be almost universal according the nature of the case and the experience. We are talking about the ordering of one's spirit in such a way that the powerful desire for the Holy, concentration on and love for it, exercise *at the same time* such dominion over one's other intellectual and moral faculties that, for example, the understanding, judgment, and imagination seek no other subjects on which to work than religion or things closely related to religion, and that the practical faculties which are directed beyond the person himself have no goal other than the spread of religion and the deepening of religious life. In my opinion, the *unequivocal* vocation for theology consists in this ordering of one's spirit, which by analogy could be called *religious genius*.

#103

Whether a person has this will be readily seen by the presence of an outward sign which infallibly accompanies it. For whenever a person's inner desire together with the faculties which serve it have been determined in a particular direction, it expresses itself outwardly as *pleasure* in and *love* for something. Delight in and eagerness for the study of theology are thus not a special requirement that must be brought to it, but rather the factual evidence that one is called to it. And the opposite is true: where that eagerness is clearly absent, theological talent is also absent, however marked one's talent in other areas may be. Occasionally it can happen that an individual's religious desire is strongly developed and his other spiritual faculties are attuned to it, but if this finds little if any expression due to his weakness of nature, then he has none of the preconditions for the study of theology except good will.

> * Likewise it can be understood from the nature of the case how it has been found through experience that even mediocre intellectual abilities, when in service of and guided by high religious aspirations, can be used scientifically and even more practically far more effectively than great talents which lack that guiding and energizing inspiration. This observation is allied to the reflection that for the vast majority of theologians practical work remains the key issue, however great the importance of studies.

#104

Where inner desire is joined to intelligence there will be found those necessary qualities which round out the student's preparation for the science because they are the immediate conditions of its fruitful study. I am referring to outward fidelity to attending lectures, enthusiasm when on his own time for thinking through what he hears and in the careful selection of his reading, and instructive conversations with other scholars. Time spent at school can only be turned to use in this way. On the other hand, one can lay the basis for a truly scientific education with zeal and application only by combining one's personal development with one's study, working one's way through the science in a well-planned and orderly manner, putting aside ready-made popular opinion for solidly based knowledge, and insisting on the utmost conceptual precision and clarity in each thing and the ultimate grounding for everything. Prudent scheduling and use of time is another very important quality for this level of study.

#105

Some general remarks about scientific study may be *à propos* here among the prerequisites. First, any student (and consequently the theologian) must presume that only the basis of scientific education is ever provided in school and that the school cannot complete, still less exhaust, science. All that can be gotten in the brief span of an academic program are a knowledge of the organic shape of the science as a whole, a knowledge of the contents of its branches in outline and in the principles which govern them, a knowledge of the sources and tools with which one can build a broader education, and lastly, the scientific spirit itself, i.e., theoretical procedures and methods and, most of all, the ability to give practical application to theory. Taking care of this prerequisite entails observing definite rules about the order of one's studies and about how much energy one should devote proportionately to various disciplines. These rules can be easily figured out from what has already been said.

#106

Furthermore, it should be obvious to anyone who wants to achieve expertise in any branch of a science or in any one of its practical applications that it is impossible to attain this level of ability in every branch and application. He will see the necessity of emphasizing those areas to which his desire for exceptional aptitude or special interest leads him or which he must master to fulfill his own future vocation within the church. Of course, he can and ought not give any one branch exclusive attention, because at this point his concern should be to gain an accurate notion of the whole science. But it ought to be important to him even at this point to make his choice and to take definite first steps in light of that choice, to assemble the necessary preparatory material and tools, etc., so that he can constantly devote his most serious study to his preparation. —Questions dealing with expertise in particular theological areas and for special purposes can be more easily discussed in the encyclopedic outline.

PART TWO

Encyclopedic Outline of the Major Branches of Theological Studies

I. Historical Propaedeutic

A.1. Biblical Study

#107

Christianity considered as a temporal phenomenon—which is both the most common and the primary way of considering it—can be viewed either as one moment in the general history of religion or as one historical totality in itself. Although he ought not to be unacquainted with the first way of viewing it, the Christian theologian treats Christianity under the second aspect: he regards it as the center of all historical religious phenomena. To understand it and present it as such, and to do so in a purely historical fashion, is the task of historical theology, or as I term it, historical propaedeutic (#64).

#108

In the historical view of Christianity the moment of its first appearance should be distinguished from those of its expansion and development. Accordingly, the description and study of Christianity in its earliest form is distinguished from the description and study of its subsequent course. Like every historical enterprise, both descriptions and both studies depend on sources and primary documents. The source and the primary document for primitive Christianity are the Bible. Hence the historical study of Christianity in its primitive form is *biblical study*.

> * In so brief a treatment of the historical perspective the reminder is scarcely needed that there can be no discussion at this point of the scientific, much less the dogmatic treatment of Christianity.

#109

The contents of the Bible—more precisely, in this case, of the New Testament—is, of course, historical in its manner of presentation. But within it there must be a distinction between what is historical of its very nature and what is only historically presented. As data, straightforward facts are historical by their nature; what are not historical by nature but historically presented are the religious and moral doctrines of Christ and the apostles as well as their institutional regulations. In accord with this distinction, *biblical history* is distinguished from *biblical doctrine*. Biblical study embraces both these subjects. Indeed, both have hitherto been classed together under the title *biblical theology*, but in its precise sense this title belongs only to the description and study of biblical doctrines. Biblical history is a title in its own right.

> * Throughout the New Testament the pointed reference of Christianity to Mosaic religion and the pre-Christian era naturally entails a similar study of the Old Testament.

#110

Christ, his person, his work, and his destiny, are clearly the proper subject of *New Testament biblical history* (as well as the center of biblical doctrine). But, as the earliest and most authentic disseminators of Christianity, his apostles and disciples are also intrinsic to the history of primitive Christianity. And ultimately so are all historical data from the time of Christ and the apostles insofar as they have any relation to primitive Christianity.

#111

Regarding the person of Christ the following are the most crucial issues: What did Christ claim about his person and identity, about his nature and his origin? What did he claim was his office? What did he say about his mission to the world, his entry into it, his role as teacher, about his teaching, and about other commands and purposes which he had to fulfill? How did he justify his claims or prove that he was what he pretended to be? What about these proofs especially: a) The proof from his spiritual gifts, abilities, understanding, knowledge, and moral and physical power? b) The proof from his maxims, behavior, and the quality and tenor of his life? c) The proof from the extraordinary things which he did? d) The proofs from his way of teaching, methods, sermons, and from the means he used to spread his teaching? e) And lastly, the proof from his ultimate destiny, from his triumph, and from its results?

#112

The theologian must also establish a historical portrait of Christ's apostles and disciples, taking special account of their personalities and background, of their apostolates, of how they discharged them, of their other deeds and their fates, etc.

* The biblical depiction of all those who heard the new religion from the lips of Christ himself, who collaborated in its spread directly or indirectly, or who stood in any relation to it, is of great importance not only for illumining the primitive history of Christianity but for correctly understanding and evaluating its doctrine.

#113

In the full treatment of biblical history reference must also be made to that branch of general history which deals with the primitive history of Christianity. For when Christianity appeared in the world as a new and wholly unique phenomenon, it encountered the world at a particular stage in its history, acted upon it in a way suitable to that stage, and was thus accepted or rejected, understood or misunderstood by the world. A great deal of the way early Christian writers and apologists wrote and expressed themselves is due to historical circumstances and the general situation of their contemporaries. So in all sorts of ways accurate study of biblical history requires familiarity with the spirit and history of that age. For this familiarity a good deal of evidence is found in the Bible itself, in both the New and the Old Testaments; what is lacking there must be filled out with the assistance of other historical works.

#114

The spirit in which this history must be done is for the most part precisely the spirit of historical investigation generally. But two considerations in particular make an important difference. The first comes from the theologian's external situation and his inner belief. As a theologian, he looks at world history, and even more biblical history, from the perspective of religion, i.e., he sees everything and so accounts for everything as being under God's governance; the effects of human freedom and of what may seem to be chance are to him the effects of a higher will, and the world's chaotic confusion is to him the drama of providence. The theologian is distinguished from the profane historian by this angle of vision through which the ordinary shape of things is transformed into something higher. This perspective, which is the biblical one, must be exercised on biblical history. The peculiar character of this history's special content creates the second consideration. This history is in large part miraculous. And the miraculous finds no place in the realm of ordinary history. Instead, ordinary history explains its phenomena by natural causes and the recognized kinds of causality. Anyone who tried to impose this sort of explanation on biblical history would be battling against the spirit in which the earliest witnesses understood that history and recorded it in scripture. It remains up to the researcher of this later age whether or not he is convinced by the miraculous character of the events which are presented as miraculous. But he should never allow himself to project his perspective onto the original witnesses and substitute his purely subjective explanatory system for that objective history which is presented as miraculous.

> * For the sake of the science it is greatly to be desired that we might have treatments of biblical history such those we have gotten of biblical theology in recent years. As a rule, the usual treatments of biblical history are designed for their own particular purposes and are of no use to the theologian.

#115

The survey of the doctrines of Christ and his apostles makes up biblical theology for the Christian. The key issue in this branch of biblical study is the correct understanding of these doctrines singly and entry into their spirit as a whole. Both are essential in order to gain accurate knowledge of the Christian religion as an objectively posited system of ideas. And biblical-historical knowledge of this system is the condition and basis for studying and presenting it scientifically as well as for personal growth and fruitful effect of these ideas in people's hearts. So biblical theology must be regarded as the foundation of the whole science.

* The relation of the New Testament to the Old is nowhere more apparent than in the doctrinal teaching of Christ and the apostles. Consequently, although the Christian theologian's first concern is always the doctrine of Christ, in order to understand it he must also be well versed in the doctrine of the Old Testament.

#116

A second requirement for biblical theology is *completeness*. The process of merely selecting and explaining the so-called *dicta probantia* for the purposes of particular theological sciences, e.g., moral theology, dogmatics, etc., is simply inadequate. For in this way only fragments of biblical theology are dealt with, never the whole and still less its spirit. This procedure certainly clarifies very few *dicta probantia* in the sense in which the term is usually used—indeed so few as to be virtually none. One and the same doctrine, indeed, one and the same idea, appears in different texts in different contexts and with certain modifications, all of which one must study if one intends to define a biblical idea or a doctrine adequately. It is thus absolutely essential for the creation of true biblical theology that each key biblical idea be taken in the full range of its various uses, as indeed ought to be the way *every* idea or doctrine is treated.

#117

The charge has been leveled against a separate study of biblical theology that within the Bible various subjects had not yet been classified separately, e.g., dogmatic theology from moral theology, etc., that ideas and doctrines are not catalogued according to any system within the Bible, and that consequently a method of procedure is employed in biblical theology which is alien to the Bible itself. Besides, it is said, biblical theology must always be redone as part of the whole study of Christian systematics. Over and above this, from the perspective of the Catholic system, the objection can be made that, since the Bible alone does not contain the whole of primitive Christian doctrine, there can be no purely biblical theology. —But these objections against the separate study of biblical theology do not stand up. For, first of all, there is absolutely no need for biblical theology to separate what is not separated in the Bible, e.g., to isolate biblical dogmatics from biblical moral theology. Nor is there any need to follow a method of procedure which is alien to the Bible in the treatment of biblical theology. For even if ideas and doctrines are not systematically arranged within the Bible, there is a system inherent in the ideas and doctrines themselves, a system which is all the more reliable because those ideas and doctrines have been revealed and are in continuity with a revelation handed down from the beginning. If we must continually come back to biblical theology in each branch throughout the whole study of Christian systematics, then this whole study finds its foundation at this point. And as for the Catholic principle, certainly it is highly desirable that we learn from biblical theology what is in the Bible and what is not in it. So in all sorts of ways a separate rigorous study of biblical theology has its own value and importance.

#118

In biblical theology is it valuable and important to distinguish the doctrine of Christ from that of the apostles and again among the apostles to distinguish the doctrine of one from that of another? —This question cannot be resolved without making some distinctions. First, it is not immediately self-evident to me that there is a difference between the doctrine of Christ and that of the apostles. For what do we mean by the doctrine of Christ? What is in the gospels. But has this not been filtered through some other mind or even through several other minds just as surely as what is in the epistles? Ultimately, if what is unique and peculiar to one apostle and the differences between his teaching and that of the others is accounted for by the claim that in his teaching he is closer to the original teaching of Christ, then I fail to see why this same kind of argument should not be applied to the gospels themselves. But then where is this original teaching to be found? Would it be whatever there is more or less general agreement on? But surely this would not come to very much. And once one allows the introduction of accident and arbitrariness as factors in these questions, they can be used to explain the agreement as the differences. So it seems to me much better to rely on good faith and consequently to accept everything as *Christian* even if one prefers not to accept everything as *apostolic*. Unless we are reluctant to recognize the miraculous, we find in the gospels and the epistles a power which guarantees that apostolic doctrine is also Christian doctrine; and so the question is resolved.

#119

It is quite another matter when the issue is the peculiar characteristics of individual apostles and evangelists. Here we are dealing with something immediately obvious, a given, not a matter of deduction. Differentiating and distinguishing among them is essential for historical accuracy. It is also the only way to understand the biblical doctrine of each of these individuals with clarity and certainty, since the doctrines taught throughout the Bible as a whole are shaped by each author in his own unique way and expounded by each in his own context with its collateral ideas and modifications. Nevertheless, even if as a result of this there is a Pauline theology, a Johannine theology, etc., a *general* biblical theology remains the key issue. For the writings of no one apostle make up the Bible but the collection of them all, and no one apostle is the canon, i.e., the source and rule of Christian doctrine, but all of them together. So what is peculiar to one gets woven into the collective fabric.

#120

Method of Biblical Study

Knowledge of biblical Christianity—biblical history and theology—may be gained in two ways: in the first, all the books of the New Testament are carefully compared with the Old, their collective meaning is sought, and with this their complete content is discovered; or in the second, similar or related data and doctrines are collected from the various writings, collated, and reduced to a common statement. The second procedure applied to all biblical data and doctrines finally yields a complete view of biblical history and theology. This second approach seems simpler and shorter.

#121

But it is also obvious that it is less certain. For the individual traits and special qualities in the ways these data and doctrines are dealt with by individual authors do not come to light in this way and so are less understood if one studies only fragments than if one reads the author fully and integrally. Precise knowledge of the Bible, however, depends especially on knowledge of these individual traits and special qualities. The author's objective presence in his style of writing and in the way he naturally puts together his thoughts makes it easier to understand his way of expressing himself. And because this eliminates the need for a lot of guesswork, it more readily avoids imposing the interpreter's own way of thinking on the biblical author. —Thus, this approach or method seems preferable.

#122

And yet in this approach one is still only dealing with biblical Christianity in a fragmentary way or with its parts taken in isolation. Finally a true overview of it is what has to be gotten. So to understand Christianity's complete history and full spirit and obtain detailed knowledge of the individual authors the second mode of procedure must be combined with the first. This can be done in such a way as to shorten the work if at the outset of the first stage—the review of the individual biblical books—each important event or idea with an accompanying note on the way it is phrased in the text were collected in a kind of biblical repository; this can be constantly expanded and enlarged under all its headings in the course of ongoing exegetical work. When all the parts of the Bible have been studied thoroughly, it should be relatively easy, first, to assemble the references to each biblical doctrine or event as variously presented in the individual books, and then to link together the fully, clearly, and precisely noted elements of biblical history and theology in their natural connections. This biblical repository may even achieve relative completeness during one's course of theological studies. Every student should work constantly at expanding and improving it.

#123

In biblical theology especially it should be obvious that the method used in assembling the elements of key ideas and linking together the ideas themselves is purely historical, i.e., it is the work of pure historical inquiry to arrange these thoughts into a natural logical order. But we are not able to make reference here to the rational principles by which these doctrines should be ordered, the consequences which must necessarily result from arranging them more artificially, etc. Nor can we establish any clear distinctions at this point among the various elements of biblical doctrines, how the science is divided up into areas, e.g., the dogmatic, the moral, the juridical, etc.

   *   Since theology which is drawn from the Bible must be *entirely biblical* by the very nature of the case, the Catholic principle of historical theology which sets tradition alongside the Bible is, here at least, inapplicable. On the other hand, an intelligent study of biblical material will pay attention to tradition, and so what is contained in tradition will surface naturally.

A.2. Exegesis

#124

The notion of exegesis, both in its general sense and in reference to the Bible and ecclesiastical tradition, has been shown to be necessary (##67–70). It stems from the fact that any historical subject—and so Christianity in its origins and later history—must depend on a tradition which, in any even moderately advanced culture, is written or comes to be written. From its beginning, Christianity has possessed a written tradition of its history, and very early this written tradition was divided up in the same fashion as was the history itself. The written sources which deal with the history of its origin are distinguished from later writings which deal with the subsequent history of Christianity; the former are called sacred scripture, the latter ecclesiastical literature. The reverence accorded the former is naturally greater than that given the latter.

#125

But no historical account can be taken directly out of its historical sources; there are certain preconditions which can be simply stated and the need for which is beyond all doubt. Since prior fulfillment of these preconditions makes it possible to interpret historical sources, which is the only way to use them correctly in doing history, and since all the studies which have been and must be pursued in this regard have the interpretation of scripture as their primary focus, the array of skills needed to treat historical subjects from their sources are known by the name of *exegetical skills*; the study of these preliminary skills is *exegesis*. —Biblical study acknowledges its dependence on exegesis as a prior scholarly tool, as a necessary condition for its being able to derive Christianity's history and doctrine from the Bible. This is what is meant by biblical exegesis.

#126

The use of scriptural sources, however, depends on two basic requirements: that one knows how to *evaluate* them and that one can *understand* them. Through evaluating them one is objectively assured of the truth of history because of the trustworthiness of the sources; through correctly understanding them one is subjectively assured of the truth of what is presented because of the accuracy of the interpretation. Correct evaluation of a source is achieved only through knowledge of its history guided by critical rules through which that history is itself correctly evaluated. Correct understanding is achieved through knowledge of the source's language guided by principles which teach how someone's thoughts can be understood from his words, both in general and in this specific instance.

> * In general, then, exegesis embraces four disciplines: textual history, criticism, philology, and hermeneutics. But one can see that these are paired off together as principles and application of principles to a given topic. Thus, criticism and hermeneutics deal with the actual theory of all exegesis; history and linguistic skills have an empirical orientation.

#127

Both in practice and theory, biblical exegesis should be regarded simply as one special form of exegesis (#70 note). It has to verify the history of its particular texts (the sacred scriptures) as to their reliability with the aid of criticism appropriate to these texts and to determine from the text's literary style its author's intention with the aid of a hermeneutics which derives from the genius of that style and that author. —The value and necessity of this whole theological discipline come from its connection to biblical study and consist in its results: correct understanding and explanation of biblical history and biblical theology.

#128

a) History of Biblical Texts

Any text has its history and its vicissitudes. It originated at a particular time and on a particular occasion. It has a particular author. Depending on our knowledge of the time and occasion of its origin and the personality of its author, and following the established laws of historical judgment, we decide whether we ought to regard the text as a reliable witness to an ancient time. —In the course of ages the text passes through the hands of many people; through their fault or just through bad luck and accident, it may be changed, distorted, mangled. Depending on our thorough knowledge of these vicissitudes we decide whether or not we ought to regard the text, even if genuine in its origin, as a true account of past events. —And finally, it can be a personal text which has no authority beyond that of its author, or it can have attained public status with genuinely authoritative weight because of general agreement based on solid grounds. In the latter case, general acceptance of the text's credibility has a weight of its own because that general agreement itself carries the force of a witness if the consensus is based on historical grounds. If the basis of the consensus is the special authority of the author, this too gives it special credibility.

#129

All of this has *special* application to the biblical texts. For they have their *special* history which must be known both for individual texts and for all of them as a collection before one is willing to pass judgment on their historical reliability and their special status. In this we see the key issues concerning the history of biblical texts. —The decision on a text's usefulness as a historical source depends on what is known of its history. If it comes from a known author to whom it can be traced back and whose name it bears, or what is even more important and why the author is significant, if it originates at the same time as the historical events which it recounts and was written by someone who was in a position to experience, evaluate, and record events or have them recorded under his direction by others with the same experience, then we call it *authentic* or *genuine*. In that case, this authenticity is the basis of its reliability and its historical status. This *authenticity* or *genuineness* is accordingly the first thing which must be established in biblical textual history and individually for each and every text (each and every biblical book).

> * The concept of authenticity varies with regard both to historical texts generally and to biblical sources particularly. Not all texts—this is true of most of the New Testament—carry their author's name on the face of them; the author is unknown and frequently cannot be discovered. In this case, authenticity, in the first of the accepted senses of the term, simply cannot be established. Often an event is not written down at the time when it happened and even less often by those who

were immediate witnesses; this is demonstrably the case with most biblical texts. Hence, even the second meaning of the term "authenticity" can scarcely be applied. Thus, biblical texts, as so very many others, must generally make do with a notion of authenticity as meaning that they originate with people deserving of trust; this rather vague sense of authenticity should be demonstrated historically insofar as it can be. How in the vocabulary of biblical believers the term *authentic* has come to have another meaning outside its accepted roots is found below.

#130

The reasons on which the genuineness of a text in the accepted sense can be educed are in part external, dependent on information and testimony of other writers, especially of the same period, and so strictly historical, or they are inherent in the text, either objectively so in its contents or subjectively so in the author. The first can be described as more evidential proofs, the latter as more inferential. The genuineness of biblical texts can and must be demonstrated through both kinds of proof, through the former as the stronger wherever possible, through the latter where the first kind of proof is inapplicable or insufficient.

#131

The history of a literary piece's origin should include, along with inquiry about the author, inquiry into what occasioned it, into its purpose, the author's mind and way of thinking, his education and other background which could have influenced his writing and be evidenced in it. In the case of biblical literature all these concerns must be even more emphasized since often it is precisely in such research that a previously unknown author and his age may be deduced or that an alleged author is established or called into question. Furthermore, these same concerns in which the *internal* reasons for genuineness properly consist, have the very greatest importance for textual interpretation.

> * Inquiries into the authenticity of the biblical books are, of course, like the subsequent inquiries into the other questions about their history, by their very nature of a *critical* sort. In the mind of the Christian theologian and in the mind and course of his science, they take on an *apologetic* color, just as in the mind of the non-Christian inquirer, they must take on a *polemical* one.

#132

The history of a literary piece especially includes all that has happened to it as these things affect its contents as a *text*. One must know whether or not the text has been altered, how, in what respects, and by whom? What editing has it undergone? What variants exist?, etc. The basic issue is obvious. Only an unchanged text or one brought as close as possible to the original through editing is true and authentic, and only such a text can yield the author's original intention. On the other hand, it is perfectly clear that insignificant changes in the text have no influence on a work's material content and that all research of this sort has as its purpose only to make sure that what is *essential* in its contents has not been altered throughout the course of the text's transmission. The *complete restoration of the original text* in the case of biblical and every other kind of literature is quite impossible, and it is not worth the effort to attempt it.

#133

So what proof of integrity means in biblical literature is clear. Furthermore, both in any particular instance and in general, this proof is to be demonstrated in the same way as the proof of authenticity. When dealing with the essential matters, or as Planck puts it, when dealing with dogmatic integrity, *each and every doubtful passage* must be specially studied and, if one intends to argue from them, justified. When dealing with the Bible as a whole, however, variants existing in all the master copies (the manuscripts) prove that no essential distortion of the Christian tradition has occurred; the impossibility of such distortion can be very sufficiently demonstrated.

#134

But the individual texts or writings in the Bible do not stand independently of one another like other literature but are bound together so that they form an indivisible whole, one single text. This bond does not consist only in the fact that they were all written by people who were closely united in a common purpose and that, from this common purpose, they all have a common content—the proclamation of the history and doctrine of Christ. But it also consists in a thoroughly positive fashion in the fact that only this collection of documents with all its parts is officially accepted by the community of Christians as the uniquely authentic written tradition of primitive Christianity. Any other documents, even if very ancient and with the same contents, are excluded from this collection of the true word of God through Christ. This is the idea of the Bible as a *canon* in the ecclesiastical sense.

> * Since the Jews already had a similar collection of canonical books before the Christians received one, the Christian and Jewish canons are distinguished even though from another point of view the two are linked as one. Cf. #109*.

#135

Since the canonicity of the biblical books has an authority distinct from and independent of their purely historical authenticity and integrity, it is of importance to know how and why they have gained that authority. From this stems a new historical inquiry which deals with all these questions. I call it *the history of the canon*, and it forms the third stage in the history of biblical literature.

#136

As is obvious, canonicity is first of all a quality added to these books. For they already existed in and of themselves before they were given their external form and were definitively assembled as a canon. That they were given this form and with it a positive extrinsic authority was the result of the common decision and common choice of a religious community or church. Only this sort of community can and must possess a canon, and it alone is able to form a canon. Thus a book is first deemed canonical because a church regards it as canonical. This can be called its *extrinsic canonicity*.

#137

But if the church accepts a book into its canon, it must have a motive for doing so and, given the purpose and significance of such a collection, this motive can only be that it regards the book as a sacred and divine book in its contents. The *intrinsic canonicity* of this book consists in the uniqueness of its content and the special reverence which is its due. And this intrinsic canonicity is the ground of extrinsic canonicity.

> * One readily sees that neither authenticity in the narrow sense (#129*) nor integrity in the fullest sense (#132) is a necessary require-

ment for the canonizing of a work. For the church does not canonize the name of its author but its content. And if at a later time something were added to the text or deleted from it, the content would not *for that reason alone* necessarily cease to be sacred and divine.

#138

Whether a given piece of literature has the character of intrinsic canonicity is a question which must be answered on the basis of either its intrinsic content or its origin. Certainly criticism can apply certain basic principles in answering the question, but when it does so it can only arrive at an approximation to the truth. The actual decision on each individual book can come only from the church and the church can base the decision only on tradition. How the synagogue formed its canon is not very clear; how the Christian church passed on the tradition on which it based the decision on its canon is much clearer.

#139

This is why the Christian church could only frame its canon gradually and could only close it later on. Framing the canon in this way gave rise to the distinction between proto- and deuterocanonical literature. But it should be observed that this distinction stems from the history of the canon and is not intrinsic to it; it comes from the way the deuterocanonical books came into the canon, not from their contents.

* Following #137, the apocrypha are actually βιβλια voθα.

#140

Once closed, the canon remains closed both negatively and positively, i.e., no book once included in it can be deleted, as is obvious, but neither can a new book be introduced into it. For even if it were absolutely certain that apostolic writings had been omitted and if their genuineness were established by the usual tools of criticism with the utmost probability, in the eyes of the church those writings would still be deficient by the standard of its most important criterion, tradition. Consequently, it could never accept such a book.

* The history to this point of the biblical books in all their facets is customarily set out in so-called "introductions" to the Old and New Testaments. Besides exclusively historical information, they ordinarily

include both application and discussion of the principles of criticism, although these still require separate treatment. Does the question of the inspiration of sacred scripture, which has clearly been part of its history and especially the history of its beginnings, have to be pursued at this point, as most recently Planck has done in his *Summary of the Theological Encyclopedia* who goes so far as to claim that it is the principal task in the history of the canon? The question is not inherent in the idea of a canon which can possess intrinsic and extrinsic canonicity (##136, 137) even if the author of the books had not been inspired. But inspiration gives higher dogmatic status to these books as sources as well as greater confidence to the belief of Christians. For these reasons and because the idea of inspiration has been attacked in various quarters, the question seems to belong to apologetics. Of course, there is the other question of whether the presumption of inspiration does not influence interpretation. But this question has to be discussed in hermeneutics.

#141

b) Biblical Criticism

No historical study—including the history of biblical literature—can be conducted without the use of criticism. Under this heading are understood first of all certain general principles and rules by which we can distinguish historical truth from falsehood. Criticism is exercised when these principles and rules are employed on any given historical question. So it is not surprising that there is a theory of historical criticism, i.e., that its principles and rules can be expressly set down and that in well-organized studies the theory of criticism must precede its exercise.

#142

Theoretically viewed, criticism is in itself a very general science and belongs by nature to the domain of philosophical sciences. When exercised on a *particular* subject, its general principles and rules must be more precisely defined in terms of this subject. Thus there are many kinds of specialized criticism. One of these is *biblical criticism*, whose historical subject is the Bible.

> *   In all criticism the specialized aspects are the result of the particular characteristics of the historical events which are its subject matter,

of the historical agents who were the active parties in this material, of the author of the narrative who is the transmitter of the history, of the historical period, etc. Thus it is clear what the specialized aspects of biblical criticism are.

** If the lack of almost any biblical criticism in earlier times was a great problem, the lack of a foundational theory of biblical criticism is no less a problem in modern times. Endless confusion in biblical history and diametrically opposed positions among critics are only the most obvious results of this deficiency in a biblical discipline which should be especially open to systematic treatment. How much has happened since Richard Simon and how little has been accomplished toward a satisfactory theory of criticism!

#143

The subject matter of biblical criticism is the history of this literature in terms of the three key issues which have been mentioned, and its task to find the truth of that history. But because the history of the Christian canon is not very hard to establish and, although thorough proof of authenticity is more difficult, this problem is resolved thanks to canonicity, textual history remains the most pressing concern for criticism and textual correction its most problematic task. The critical perspective is all the more indispensable since looking on these books as canonical can no more render scrutiny of the books unnecessary than their canonical quality can protect them from the vicissitudes common to every other kind of literature.

* Any worry which the immensity of critical work on the Bible may inspire in theologians is dispelled by reflecting that no distortion has taken place in the text in any essential regard and that corrections of non-essentials are of no immediate importance for theology.

#144

In recent times a distinction has been drawn between lower and higher criticism, but there is no unanimity on the idea. By analogy to the way these terms are employed in other sciences, less rigorous tasks would have to be assigned to lower criticism and more rigorous to higher criticism; yet textual emendation, which is for the most part as demanding as any other task, is often ascribed to lower criticism. Others have dealt with the question as one of relative importance of the material and so have ascribed to higher criticism questions involving authenticity and the origin and early history of biblical sources. And still others have added to the importance of the material the distinctive mode of operation and tools of criticism, which in ordinary criticism are simply given (historical data) but in higher criticism are reflective and comparative and even speculative. This last use of the terms may in fact be the historically correct one, for the originators of higher criticism began in that way. —A careful theory of biblical criticism has to clarify this notion.

#145

Tools and evidence in criticism, which determine critical procedures, are either simply given and historical or consequent on what is given, drawn from it, built upon it. The first can be called historical evidence, the second philosophical evidence. The first is like witnesses speaking from other times and in other tongues who testify to the primitive history, such as manuscripts, traditions, quotations, etc., whose value as a rule is decided by their antiquity. The philosophical evidence is like an invocation of the spirit of the ancient author to speak on his own behalf and give testimony—through compiling and comparing his thoughts, the character of his language, his literary style, etc.

> *   Older criticism confined itself mostly to evidence of the first sort and was deficient even in this. Modern criticism made good use of such evidence at first, and after it had done so began almost to disdain this resource and to seek something more. The strictly historical route now satisfies few, and yet its tools lead directly to the fact which is sought. Now facts must be established first of all by the method of combination and what one wants to find must be sought in these combinations by deduction. But in these complicated procedures there is greater chance of error. Indeed, this aversion to the straightforwardly empirical and this complication of simple operations into multiple steps are a product of the age, like so many other examples of the same sort. They are an integral part of the same phenomenon.

#146

c) Biblical Philology

In dealing with a biblical source, even if one grants that all important steps in its evaluation have been done correctly and one now has the source exactly as it was when it was first written and so, from the historical point of view, a perfectly unimpeachable source but written in a foreign language, the understanding of its language is still a necessary condition for making use of it. Training and deeper study in the languages in which the biblical sources were written are thus necessary for exegetical studies.

> * Translations of the Bible cannot make skills in biblical languages superfluous. A) No translation perfectly corresponds to the original, least of all biblical translations, given the many peculiarities of the original languages and of the authors of the books. B) Only the originals have *actual* canonical authority. C) Without study of the original languages no translations, let alone good ones, are possible.

#147

The original language of the New Testament books, which are sacred scripture specifically for Christians, is a kind of Greek dialect which was originated by the Jews in order to translate their sacred writings into Greek and so to transform Jewish ideas and formulae into Greek expressions and which was further developed by later Jewish writers who wished to write in Greek. It is a dialect which the New Testament authors found in sacred scripture in their time and which was largely already familiar to their contemporaries but which they had still to expand with many new forms and idioms because of the unusualness and novelty of Christian thought. So, the New Testament's language, taken as a whole, is entirely unique and not to be learned and understood from the septuagint translation nor from the Greek books of the Old Testament with the addition of Philo and Josephus, and even less from the classical tongue of the Greeks. Specialized study of the New Testament authors is required to understand it.

> * As great as the difficulties of this Hellenistic language are, they are still significantly eased by two facts, that by far the largest part of its elements is already found in the Greek Old Testament and that naturally the same content (Christianity and its doctrines) is discussed by several writers and in several books by the same writer.

#148

The study of the language of the Old Testament presents still greater problems. Not only is it a language unique within the ancient world, it was never very widely spoken and long ago died out. The events and customs that are described in it, the whole perspective and thought-world in which the authors approached their material, come from a time far older than other languages and literatures, and this gives the whole structure of the language a peculiar character and is reflected in its poverty of words and literary remains.

> * An *adequate* knowledge of Old Testament texts also requires knowledge of dialects closely related to Hebrew; a *full* knowledge demands acquaintance with other semitic languages as well. For they are a specific family of languages with branches spread throughout the northern half of Asia.

#149

Since knowledge of oriental languages is not limited to grammar alone but has to include the whole spirit of the languages, and since the spirit of a language comes from the spirit of a people, from the level of their culture and their way of thinking, it can be seen that for entry into the spirit of the language of the Old Testament (and this holds for related dialects as well) other studies are needed which are not philological in the strict sense but historical. Because they deal with the history of customs and culture among ancient peoples, they are called *archeological*. There is a biblical archeology, and it is an indispensable resource for biblical linguistic studies.

#150

In general terms biblical archeology embraces natural history and human history in those ages and climes from which the biblical sources come. More particularly it includes knowledge of those circumstances and characteristics in which the spirit of peoples and nations finds special expression and which in turn, as distinctive cultural elements, form that spirit, as for example, domestic and civil arrangements, religion and art, etc.

> * To the extent that a people's way of life and thought are always modified by the influence exerted by the culture of neighboring peoples or of those with whom they are in some way affiliated, attention must also be paid to this in the study of antiquity.

#151

The difficulty of pursuing such studies may be grasped if one considers their breadth on the one hand and the paucity of resources on the other. But much has already been achieved by comparing and assembling hints about the ancient world scattered through the Old Testament writings, and much else by consulting and comparing the many very ancient relics from early Egyptian, Persian-Chaldean, and even Indian antiquity (#150*). Much can also be learned in this regard from the current state of those lands and regions where the history of the Old Testament took place. For in their dominant features the character of lands and climates does not alter so significantly even over millennia that their present appearance bears no resemblance to how they looked in antiquity and that the way of life of contemporary inhabitants has no similarity to that of earlier peoples.

#152

d) Biblical Hermeneutics

But even if the purpose of all linguistic studies is and can only be to understand literature, that understanding is still not achieved by knowledge of a language alone. For not only does the individual word by itself have multiple meanings, this polysemic quality is still more increased by its connection with other words. And this is how the author is able to display endless variety in his thoughts and to express a concept or idea in many ways and so with the greatest variety. And so the precise statement of his concepts and ideas—*his meaning*—is not immediately given by an author's words. It has to be discovered; at least, it often is discovered.

#153

The art which teaches us how to find it is hermeneutics, the art of interpretation. By its nature it is as wide as criticism and must be based on the laws through which the human mind arrays its thoughts in words or actually thinks in words. —Since every writer has not only his own ideas and thoughts but his own manner of speaking in which he clothes them as well, we have in each writer a unique instance of the laws of thinking in words. And so the interpreter must become familiar with this unique instance. Thus there comes the notion of a special hermeneutics. Biblical hermeneutics is such a special hermeneutics and must base its rules on the knowledge of the particular characteristics of biblical authors and their manner of expression.

* The general principles of hermeneutics are certainly attainable by rigorous deduction, and principles ought also to be deduced in special

hermeneutics as well. But in its application to a particular author and style of language the principle becomes a simple rule, which throws the interpreter back completely on his own tact and genius in explaining particular instances, i.e., in other words, literary interpretation is an art.

#154

Hermeneutics is thus one of the exegetical disciplines which actually form the scriptural interpreter, indeed, one of those which do so most directly. Viewed in this way, it is the last in order but the first in importance. For even were one to imagine that, as for linguistic studies, a theologian could be satisfied with using biblical translations and, as for historical studies and criticism, could confine himself to the opinions of approved biblical scholars (a status which can indeed be attributed to certain individuals because of their qualifications and the church's regard for their work), it still remains absolutely essential for him to know how to interpret the Bible for himself, just as it is ultimately for every reader of the Bible, even uneducated ones.

#155

Hermeneutics, or more precisely the application of its rules, is also the most difficult of these disciplines—because the authors to be interpreted wrote among a foreign people, in a past and in some cases long past age, with little or no erudition, for the most part without anything other than a religious background, and so in a style of expression very dark and obscure to us. Add to this that a large part are merely occasional writings and that therefore most of the circumstances surrounding their creation and their intention are unknown and must first be learned from the writings themselves.

> * In interpreting nature, observations and experiments assist us; in interpreting a living person's speech, the use of questions and discussion assists us. Understanding a dead person's communication can be facilitated in none of these ways. But just as we interpret the vestiges of an earlier (physical) stage of the world from the living phenomena of its present state, and many times interpret the statements of a deceased person from the explanations of those who heard his living words, so in Catholic exegesis there is an analogous way of interpreting the Bible. It is the definitive way, but we cannot discuss it further at this point.

#156

The account of the principles of biblical hermeneutics does not really belong here, but because most recently great confusion has prevailed in this field as well as in criticism, some allusion to these principles will not be beside the point. —Because language is indispensable both for thinking and for expressing one's thoughts to others, and consequently one *can* only form one's thoughts in one's language as it exists and *must* do so when speaking to others, the strong objective character of speech is the universal law for writers in recording their thoughts and the universal law for expositors in recovering those thoughts from the words of scripture. Because of the *objectivity* of language and because of the *all-embracing way* in which it limits the writer, the principle of *grammatical* interpretation is the universal and, in this respect, the supreme and primary principle of interpretation.

#157

But there is nothing so objective and so all-embracing that the subjective power of the mind and the individuality of the will cannot subdue and modify it. And so all languages, all the meaning and significance of words, gradually change. For this reason every language has its history. The universal principle of grammatical interpretation undergoes qualification or rather takes on more precise definition by reference to the history of the language, which is not independent of the history of the people who speak it. But because the grammatical principle still maintains its sway over individual authors even when they modify the language's use, one must maintain *the more general as the rule* and recognize that a writer will think in the mind-set of a given period, nation, and audience and will write in a way that accords with them. This leads to the principle of *historical* interpretation, using that term in its truest and most characteristic sense.

* One can see that the so-called principle of *accommodation* is precisely the historical principle, not merely one application of it.

#158

But if this latter principle is not qualified by yet a third it would end by contradicting and negating itself. For there would be nothing to prevent treating any author as though he were simply a product or organ of his age, and so one would fail to realize that only in the most general sense can an age, the mind-set of that age, a particular style of language, etc., be determinative. When this latter point is kept in mind, it must be acknowledged that in the great number of thoughtful people and authors there may, at least from time to time, be some who move into a new realm of ideas and who make available to their contemporaries previously unimagined achievements of the mind in freshly minted words or in a new way of using old words and so become the creators and teachers of a new age. Allowing for this possibility, the question must be raised in interpreting an author whether he may not be such a person. And since such a person cannot rightly be expounded simply on the ground of the ordinary use of language or by his period and its style but only in his own terms, I call the principle introduced here *individual* interpretation.

> * This principle, since it qualifies the *most general* and likewise the *more general*, is the most definite and *therefore* the highest. But the answer to the question above must precede its application. And although the basis for this will be found in the substance and content of a person's writings, nevertheless his personal history and that of his opinions will orient the interpreter in these matters. For quite apart from someone's personality, it is both a decisive and understandable argument that if he did not appear as a sign of contradiction to the customary ideas of the run-of-the-mill teachers and students of his own day, he is unlikely to have inaugurated a new day in history.

#159

These three principles are fully universal. So they also hold good in biblical hermeneutics without regard to how those books are regarded or what authority may be attributed to their authors. If the books of the Bible are accepted as what they claim to be, namely a divine revelation, the word of God which was *given* to their writers, then still another unique principle of interpretation must be added, especially on account of the New Testament's relation to the Old. Of course, this has no effect on the author's (subjective) meaning, the way in which he received and expressed the word of God which was given to him; as always in words, sentences, etc., there can only be *one* meaning, and it is to be found through the three principles discussed above. But it does have an effect on the (objective) import of revealed ideas. Here another principle of interpretation must be involved: that ideas given in revelation have to be given in a form which is, of course, appropriate to a particular time and heard in a way suitable to that time, but that their full import, their power to inspire religious life and their mission to do so, cannot be reduced to that particular historical form nor to the agency of *one* person. All revelation is multiple in its meaning and its form.

> * It cannot be denied that Christ and the apostles have given to numerous Old Testament passages a meaning which is demonstrably not in accord with the sense of the ancient author—not the historical sense. But it is certainly in accord with the meaning of revelation and expresses it as it had to be expressed.

#160

To be sure, interpretation always deals first with individual passages, but its purpose is to understand the whole. Now, since an idea always lies at the root of the whole, the aim of any interpretive work must be correctly to understand and explain each individual thought of the writer as an organic part of the whole and in relation to the idea of the whole. At the outset a particular passage of a book may be this whole, subsequently the book itself, then more broadly the collected works of a biblical author, and finally the total Bible as a canon. One can see how the canon emerges as a necessary idea.

#161

Engaging in interpretation is a tightly controlled and by no means casual operation. The interpreter must put himself completely in the author's position, must transform himself into the author, so to speak, and then construct anew what the author created originally; this is called reconstruction. The vocation of the interpreter for this work consists in the ability to transform himself into this very different author. So the art of interpretation requires a special talent, and principles and rules can in no way make up for its lack.

> * From the aims and experience of interpretation is derived the modern definition of hermeneutics: the art of understanding an author's thoughts in their relation to the idea of the whole and of reconstructing his act of authorship.

#162

Method of Exegetical Study

Since by their nature all exegetical disciplines belong under the heading of philological-historical studies and are distinguished only by their orientation to Christian theology as their special end, the most basic precepts dealing with the method of these studies are the same as those which generally govern the study of history and linguistics. Nevertheless, in these special cases there are particular rules for particular disciplines, partly to govern the method of their study, partly to clarify the relation between the general principles which everyone has to know and the particular principles which only some people are required to know.

#163

Now, as regards the history of the sacred books one by one and together as the canon, the latter can be dealt with much more easily and quickly than the former. The history of the biblical canon, i.e., the history of its formal construction, has few problems. Over the construction and history of the Hebrew canon there lies to be sure great obscurity which will never be resolved. But for the Christian theologian this does not have the importance that it must have for the scholar who is a devout Jewish believer. As for the relationship of the New Testament to the Old, however, it is enough to know that the Jewish sacred books were recognized as sacred by Christ and his disciples; it is not difficult to decide which among them are to be counted in the collection of these books. For without further inquiry, the Jewish canon was accepted by the first Christian believers in the form in which they had received it from the apostles.

#164

The history of the individual books is more difficult, not only because so many kinds of literature are found in them and they originally come from a wide variety of sources but also because it is not easy to determine the time they were written or their authors and so their authenticity, due to the lack of sufficient information. But anyone who wants to do a full and precise study of the history of the biblical books will find the necessary resources assembled in the critical apparatus from ancient and modern times, in polyglot works and certain editions of the oldest biblical translations, and in collections of variants and critical recensions of the texts. Anyone who decides to become acquainted with the results of these studies will find them in the very numerous introductions to the Old and New Testaments which have been published.

#165

Nevertheless, the immense amount of data which has been assembled is not without need of correction, nor are the conclusions drawn from these data or the opinions on the history of the Bible found in the above-mentioned works in full agreement with one another. The necessary consequence of this for the student of the science is that he should accept neither data nor opinions at face value and without further test but for the moment ought to note them so that he can subsequently make his own decision about them.

> * In general, with regard to the history of biblical books, one must note well the following two principles: first—not to be upset by even the most daring claims of modern critics. For just as in an earlier time the lower criticism, so now the higher criticism in its turn must be exercised on all the biblical books, and there is no doubt whatsoever that they will come through this second trial as well as they did the first. —Second, canonicity is completely independent of the demonstrable authenticity of any book of religion or morality. And so, as Schleiermacher has said, even if it could be shown that particular writings have authors other than those to whom they had been ascribed, this would be no ground whatsoever for removing them from the canon.[36] For, as he noted, we cannot entertain the idea that the early church came to mistaken conclusions about essential points.

#166

In light of the whole-hearted dedication one has to bring to this field of exegesis, the conclusion is clear that assembling the data and pertinent information for verifying sacred scripture or thoroughly examining them will not be a job for everyone. It can only be done by people who make such studies their life's work. But one ought to require of any student that he be prepared to test opinions formed by others on these issues. But this demands clear fundamental principles and good critical theory; everyone must try to equip himself with these.

#167

One should begin biblical linguistic studies before entering into theological study (#89). These prior studies must extend to everything connected with grammar and vocabulary and so with definition of the meaning of words. Only the higher study of languages, biblical philology properly so-called, which introduces one into the language's mind-set, its characteristic qualities, its style of speech for all kinds of subjects, its various modes of expression, etc., is included in the rank of academic studies. But a foundation can be laid in these prior studies for the higher study of languages which must subsequently be built on them.

#168

The first step which ought reasonably to be taken toward this end is to avail oneself of others' earlier labors and to gather necessary information from them. Certainly there is no dearth of these scholarly aids now after so much long-continued research in biblical linguistics. Extremely valuable studies and collections are available in grammar and vocabulary, in the forms and structure of Old Testament languages, and in the various dialects which gave birth or contributed to the language of the New Testament. This is also true of ancient history which clarifies ancient languages as well as biblical chronology and geography, the tools of that history. Using them requires the same intellectual industry as expanding and adding to them.

#169

What can be required of every theologian in terms of biblical linguistic study is sufficient knowledge of the basic languages that he is in a position to read and understand sacred scripture in them and to evaluate its translation. Of course, the degree to which he does this will depend on each individual's industry and ability. In particular, full knowledge of the language of the Old Testament is attained only through knowledge of its related dialects. But just as only a few will succeed at this in view of the abilities and background required, so too only those who feel called to make significant contribution to the science need to undertake it.

#170

As regards the actual art of exposition, the first and foremost rule for each person must always be that he is expected to do his own interpretative work. And the whole method of study in hermeneutics must be geared and set up in accord with this guiding rule. Thus the first and unavoidable task for the student in this regard is to obtain knowledge of the rules of general and special hermeneutics through lecture courses and private study and to learn how to account for them according to *established principles*. Anyone who simply tries to abstract these rules from examples will end up not only, as Schleiermacher says, forever following some odd and unclear feeling[37] but will also remain forever dependent on authority—which is opposed to the primary condition of all interpretation, namely its independence—and, especially in present circumstances, will be forever in doubt as to whom he should take as his example.

#171

In other respects, independence in actual exegesis and in its principles and rules by no means excludes the budding student in hermeneutics from making use of aids which facilitate his study of the art and which are available to him in various handbooks, glossaries, and annotated editions of the whole Bible and other large biblical works, in commentaries on the Old and New Testaments separately, in explanations and paraphrases of particular books and in many other works of this sort. Only he must never forget in all of this his own independence of judgment and the need to check the interpretations of others.

#172

Distinctions between the general and the particular, between what anyone has to be able to do and what pertains to higher levels of mastery, do not apply here as they do in other exegetical studies. The reason has already been given above in #154. But because interpretation of scripture is an art and an art demands special talent, distinctions coming from genius and artistic sensitivity or their absence must apply. So each one must certainly strive for full mastery; his efforts will undoubtedly teach him how closely he approximates it.

#173

The *literal* interpreter of scripture is educated in all the philological-literary studies whose subjects and methods have been discussed to this point. But above the letter of the Bible hovers the Spirit, that Spirit who in an hour of religious ecstasy laid hold of the author's heart, allowed him to gaze into the depths of the Holy and led him to proclaim what he had seen. To be sure, this Spirit formed the literal sense of his words, but the Spirit is not contained in the letter and is not confined by it. Therefore, although the sense of the words may be uncovered by the skills of scholarship, the superintending Spirit is not to be derived from the letter. This means that there is a higher understanding of the Bible, based not on the flesh but on the Spirit; it is mediated only by that same Spirit in the heart who originally quickened the authors as they wrote. Apart from the Spirit, only the shell will be understood, not the kernel. —So here again the secret of interpretation turns out to be the art of transforming oneself into the author and of reconstructing the act of his writing (#161), but now the act is far nobler than a matter of grammar and the art is a holy one. The religious sense, and certainly the Christian religious sense, is an essential quality both for a good theologian generally (#102) and for the exegete.

> * Herein lies especially the basis for the well-known distinction between scholarly and devotional readings of scripture. That the latter can exist without the former *in fact* must be presumed both from longstanding experience and from the recent attempt at a general diffusion of reading the Bible. And so too one must presume what is a kind of miracle, that the Spirit awakens in unlearned but religious breasts not only the original sentiment but the original idea as well; otherwise different religious images would have to occur to the current reader than the original writers had placed in their words. But be that as it may, the positive science, whose task is to establish and preserve the original idea, cannot renounce historical and so scholarly exegesis. And even practically oriented interpretation finds no problem with this because it wants to be sure that it is in contact with the actual—historical—channel in order to accomplish its work.

B. Historical Theology

#174

Because in the historical view of Christianity the moment of its first appearance and its earliest form can be distinguished from the period of its wider expansion and its development, biblical study can be distinguished from what has already been termed *biblical theology*. The accurate understanding of all historical phenomena in the period mentioned in all their relationships is the subject of this study and its exposition the subject of this science. Since the sum of all these phenomena, Christianity come to objective reality, is generally called the church, its history is also church history in the broad sense, and so its study is *the study of church history*.

* It is clear that, in spite of this division for the sake of historical study, the primitive history and the further course of Christianity are in fact only *one history*, just as Christianity is itself only one reality in the ordinary sense. Consequently, for knowledge of Christianity its further course is a subject just as important and necessary as its primitive history. —This is the Catholic view of historical theology.

#175

As to the fundamental view taken toward all the relevant phenomena, the higher idea of history demands that they be seen as the straining and struggling of one single principle, of *one living force* which spreads beneath the forces of the age to take its own distinctive shape, which *expands beyond itself* and draws all things into its orbit, forming into itself what is open to such formation and destroying what is in contradiction to it. All great phenomena of history must be viewed in this way. But Christianity especially has taken this view of itself, since it precisely and exactly describes the force of life from which all its developments are derived and which, to differentiate sharply what is proper and essential to this spirit from the spirit of the preceding age, it sets in opposition to the latter. Any historical treatment and explanation of the phenomena of Christianity based on another principle than that presented here contradicts Christianity; it is unchristian and untheological.

* The correct application of this principle extends first of all to the larger divisions of history, of course, but it also influences one's judgment and explanation of particular events as well.

#176

Because, when it began to develop outward, the spirit of Christianity encountered another spirit present already in the world, it could not expand beyond itself without bumping into this spirit, and that in a hostile way. The spirit of the world reacted against it in a similar fashion—and so the history of Christianity appears at its beginning and in the long period afterward as the history of a struggle between two spirits of the age for the lordship of the world. Thus, although it is purely Christian in principle, in its phenomena this history is the joint product of two elements. And its contents are divided accordingly.

#177

Specifically, the phenomena in which the life-giving power of Christianity is freely evidenced and in which its spirit is immediately expressed and embodied in external reality are the immediate and proper subject matter of this history. The content of these phenomena can be called the *internal history* of historical Christianity because in it its inner reality has become most completely visible. By contrast, the phenomena in which Christianity is seen struggling with or overcoming the spirit of the world are the subject matter of this history only because and to the degree that Christianity has come into contact with the world and that these phenomena have resulted. The content of these phenomena can be called the *external history* of Christianity because they already had concrete existence and so Christianity could only exert its power on these given realities and form its spirit within them. It is understood, however, that even in this external history the spirit of Christianity must be exhibited as well as in the internal history.

#178

In its struggle with the world or its external history, Christianity has to be understood in part as undergoing trial, or at least as still embattled, and in part as advancing toward its victory. From this perspective the questions must be raised, "What has Christianity suffered within the world, and what has it achieved?" These questions are answered through the history of its *vicissitudes* and its *actions*. For the world's reaction is the opposition which it has placed to Christianity's introduction and spread. Christianity here is seen as both active and passive. But once it had overcome the world's opposition, it began peacefully to move out into the world in all directions and to reorder the state of the world in accord with its new spirit. It here is seen as more active than passive.

> * Christianity's external history is, of course, also part of the subject matter of general world history. But the general religious point of view is usually not the one adopted by someone in explaining secular history, nor is the particular Christian point of view what he ought to adopt. And the events which make up that external history are so lost among the events of universal history that no full and comprehensive view of the one is possible in conjunction with the other. Even apart from the uniqueness of historical theology's point of view (#175), a full knowledge demands that the external aspects of the history of Christianity be treated from its special perspective.

#179

In the internal history of Christianity, where its spirit is freely and immediately acknowledged and takes form, the elements of that spirit and the forms in which it developed—which were not yet clearly defined in the Bible (#117)—are now distinguished from one another and made special subjects of historical investigation and scientific construction. On the one hand, Christianity has formed itself into a fully defined system of religious ideas and, on the other, into a fully defined community of persons in which those ideas are continually realized. The internal history of Christianity thus divides into the *history of Christian ideology* (history of Christian doctrine in the widest sense) and the *history of the institutions of the Christian church*.

> * In working through them and in their conceptual apparatus these two may be separated, but they are in themselves inseparable. For the ideas are taken from the church and are only real within it; and the church is established through the ideas and formed by them. Therefore, the exposition of the ideas and their history can be done only from the perspective of the church and for its sake (#54), and in the (empirical) situation of the division of the Christian church into many institutional churches, from the perspective of each particular one and for its sake.

B.1. External History of Christianity

#180

Both chronological order and the way things are connected require that one first make oneself familiar with the *history of the vicissi-*

tudes of Christianity before turning one's attention to its effects on the world. To this history belong all the notable events which make clear how Christianity—as a religious system and a church—spread in the world at large and among particular peoples and lands and how it was established and maintained. Thus it is the history of Christianity's introduction, expansion, and continuance in the world.

> * The division of this history into a general branch and various special branches is already implicit in what has been said.

#181

The most important points which historical inquiry (and exposition) must note here are, first, the state of the world at large and of certain nations, especially in the time immediately before the introduction of Christianity. For their circumstances, especially in religion, morals, and intellectual culture, determined Christianity's way of relating to these nations and so what happened to it among them. It is impossible to understand the beginning of a new era—and this is what Christianity established wherever it found entry—apart from the character of the preceding age.

#182

Second, this external history must examine the power and the means by which Christianity gained its entrance, expanded, and maintained itself. What is relevant here are the history and an account of the character of Christianity's first heralds, generally and with special reference to particular times and nations, as well as the aids which they used for their purposes, their teaching abilities, methods, and so forth.

> * From the disproportion of the apparent strengths and means, about which we certainly do not know enough due to lack of information, to their results, a proof has been derived for the cooperation of a higher power and providence in favor of Christianity—I think quite rightly.

#183

And finally, the third point is the opposition which Christianity encountered, its causes and effects, how Christianity withstood it, and by what means it overcame it. On the other hand, what favorable external circumstances contributed to its expansion and preservation must also be investigated and specified. These are the key points through which the vicissitudes of Christianity become clear. Obviously the unique inner quality of its teachings and the way they resonated within the human heart ought not to be overlooked in this.

* With regard to the opposition which Christianity encountered, we have various special branches of history dealing with particular consequences of that opposition, such as the histories of persecutions, of martyrs, of apologists for Christianity, etc.

#184

Christianity's effects on the world and within it include all noteworthy changes which it produced by its entry and even more after its gentle subjugation of the whole human condition and which can be seen by comparing an earlier age with the Christian era. These changes may be noted and distinguished in the same way as human affairs generally: to wit, as all human situations and relations are either *simply human* or *civil*, so at least as a starting point it is conceivable that Christianity would have affected both kinds of relations in human life and brought about changes in both.

* As with the vicissitudes of Christianity, here too there is a place for the distinction of a general history and various special histories with reference to particular nations and centuries.

#185

Among simply human concerns, religion and morality, the worship of God and ethical mores, are preeminent. On these Christianity had to exert an even greater and more decisive impact, since it claimed to be a religious-moral system with the quickening of faith and love as its twofold principle and announced openly to all its intention to bring about a fundamental improvement in these all-important areas. —The transformations worked by Christianity in humanity's religious opinions and practical moral principles are obvious in the Christian ideas which have to be compared with those which generally prevailed earlier, at least in key respects, to see the great gain which humanity has received. What cannot be seen in these key Christian ideas, however, because it is exclusively the subject of history, is the impact these key Christian ideas have had on human hearts and the history of piety and morals among Christian people resulting from this. So this constitutes the first and most important division of the history of Christianity's effects.

#186

But as all functions of the intellectual life touch on one another, the changes effected by Christianity in religious and moral ideas must also entail similar changes in the whole education of the mind through science and art. To be sure, the influence of Christianity here did not seem significant in the beginning. Not only did it allow the earlier culture of the ancient world to collapse under the assaults of the barbarians, it positively contributed to its collapse, and centuries passed before a new culture arose on the ruins of the old. But that ancient culture, rooted in a totally different spirit, had to pass away together with its peoples if the new culture rooted in the spirit of Christianity was to unfold; the new religion had first to spur new peoples to great deeds before their spirit could engage its lofty and beautiful themes and produce speculative thought and cultural impetus. The influence of Christianity on science, art, and literature, destructive at the outset and only later constructive, is therefore a significant branch of this part of its history.

#187

No less important and interesting is historical study of Christianity's influence on civil life and its organization. For even if Christianity does not seem to have much concern with these issues, judging from its earliest history and the tenor of its doctrines considered one by one, nevertheless, even apart from the influence any religion has on the life of the state, in the universalism of Christianity's orientation as contrasted with the narrow nationalism of all earlier religions there is an important reason for the fact that it could no longer serve the nation or the society in the way earlier religions had. A certain cosmopolitanism characteristic of the spirit and essence of Christianity is one of its chief qualities. And if in terms of civil life it has thus done damage to patriotism in the ancient sense, it has by contrast rendered the greatest service to the humanity of each individual. And what it has contributed to the development of European national unity and to the breakup of the old universal monarchies over half of the Christian peoples ought not to be overlooked. Wherever its worldview is dominant in government, these effects must follow. History shows how it has accomplished this, as it also shows why these results have not occurred in those cases when they have not.

#188

But Christianity has also exercised its influence within states and must so exercise it. It therefore belongs to the history of its effects to show to what degree it has improved the spirit of the laws and also gradually modified the laws which have so largely been taken over by Christian states from antiquity, to what degree it has altered the situations of particular classes, estates, and corporations within the state or even helped to form new ones, and what influence it has had on constitutions and forms in general. Finally, this study can not avoid the question of what Christianity has contributed to the general furtherance of human happiness and to the perfection of our race.

* Until now most of these important topics have not been investigated specifically or in detail, just as we have no general pragmatic history of Christianity's effects on the world. Theologians do not customarily count these areas of inquiry as part of historical theology, but they are certainly part of historical knowledge and part of a correct assessment and evaluation of Christianity, and in fact there is more greatness and edification in these histories than in whole libraries of ordinary works of church history. Observations on many of the subjects mentioned here are contained in Tittmann's[38] book, *On the Relation of Christianity to the Development of the Human Race*, Leipzig, 1817.

B.2. Internal History of Christianity

#189

The spirit of Christianity as a world phenomenon is based on its ideas, and so it is expressed immediately (#177) in the progressive development, elaboration, and unification of these ideas into a unity which is regarded as the common property of the Christian world and the common doctrine of Christians. The history of these doctrines thus forms the first principal division of the internal history of Christianity. But as a system of images, any doctrine, when it has become a living belief common to many, must influence their life in all its forms and create a single life which they share and which in accord with its character is called the (Christian) *way of life* and, as a fully objective and completed phenomenon, the (Christian) *fellowship*—the *church*. The history of this Christian communal life thus necessarily forms the second principal division of the internal history of Christianity.

* Since doctrine (in itself an abstraction) and lifestyle (as a result of doctrine) exist only in the church, and since the church alone as a union and organization of persons is an actual phenomenon, so the history of doctrines and lifestyle can only be set forth with reference to this organization and its changes; and so the whole internal history of Christianity can be called *church history*.

#190

Insofar as the history of doctrines especially is concerned, its study must pay particular attention to and make use of the principle laid out in #175 for the general history of Christianity, i.e., the history of Christian doctrines must be viewed as the continuous and uninterrupted action of Christian ideas on the human mind; through this action and through the results which it effects in the human mind these Christian ideas ceaselessly strive to develop and transcend themselves in an effectiveness and consistency which is rooted in the very nature of Christianity. If this principle is overlooked, there is no common thread in the history of doctrines to link its data together; they then become no more than a motley mix and whirl of human opinions to which the adjective "Christian" cannot be applied with any justification.

#191

The internal consistency in the development of Christian ideas, however, in no way excludes external influences and occasions. These are usually necessary requirements for a formative process to proceed inwardly; and since history undeniably demonstrates external influences on the progressive formulation of Christian doctrines, the second major task of the history of these doctrines is to trace those influences and to show what part they have had in the actual formation and development.

#192

Since the ideas of Christianity are by their nature living realities, they originally spread abroad as living realities—through the living word—and through all centuries have been communicated in the same way in the church through the agency of the teaching office established by Christ. And so the scripture which begins and is preserved along with this living tradition must be external to that tradition and thus act on the development of doctrine as an external factor. Throughout its history the study of the Bible has had an impact on doctrine and has had that impact in those respects in which it was energetically pursued. Thus its influence must be noted and observed throughout. —But all ideas, and so Christian ideas as well, mutually affect one another, and so whatever ideas, especially of a philosophical or scientific character, have existed or have recently been discussed among people must act on Christian doctrines as external stimuli. Therefore, what the influence of the whole scientific thought-world in any age has been on their development must be investigated and determined. —Only ideas can truly affect ideas, and so if history should show that other alien factors, e.g., political power, external force, etc., have seemed to influence Christian doctrines, these do not deserve to be taken into account, since by their nature these factors can only be and actually have been superficial and without permanent effect.

> *   History demonstrates that when a prevalent style of philosophy has, in its general ideas, exerted an important influence on the formation of doctrine, biblical studies have been eclipsed, and vice-versa. It is apparent that the human mind can not pursue the same subject simultaneously by way of speculation and by way of historical investigation.
>
> **   It is customary to explain as detrimental to Christian doctrine and even as corruptive the influence which philosophical ideas have undeniably had in all periods and not only in the so-called Platonic fathers. But aside from the inescapable influence of the prevalent philosophy which cannot be less than that of the whole cultural ambience, the question simply comes to this: are those philosophical ideas in the spirit of Christianity and are they in harmony with it? Only if they are not can corruption emerge. The formulation of Christian doctrines by means of ideas drawn from the wider culture is not corruption but rather the precise task of science.

#193

Not every development or formulation of doctrine, however, whether through historical examination of the Bible or through speculation on ideas, is in accord with the spirit of Christianity. An individual or individuals by whom some modification of doctrine is first introduced can err. The spirit of Christianity, however, and of its doctrine is always present in the community, in the church. Hence it excludes any modification contrary to this spirit as *de facto innovation* (the invasion of what is foreign and not originally posited in the spirit of Christianity). So there arise in the history of doctrine, along with consistent and legitimate developments, divergences toward heterogeneous formulations which, if they seek out and win their own spheres of influence, become *schisms*. Thus the history of heresies and schisms belongs to the history of Christian doctrine not only for the sake of historical completeness but because the spirit of the church is most consciously manifested in sloughing off what is alien to it, in the same way as the foreign element which sets itself up in opposition to the spirit of the church attains its own self-awareness.

> * The historian *per se* has to engage in a critique of the foreign element as well as of all new formulations not for its own sake but in order to explain its causes and effects. Were he to do so for its own sake, he would become a dogmatic theologian.

#194

Theology as science distinguishes within Christian doctrine the theoretical aspect from the practical and, of course, treats each in an appropriate way. But in historical inquiry and historical explanation where one is dealing with the initial empirical apprehension of the whole of Christian doctrine, this distinction does not hold. For the two doctrines, theoretical and practical, are mutually explanatory, and changes in practical doctrines especially are simply inexplicable without recourse to the history of theoretical doctrines, as may be easily seen from the examples of the most important changes in moral teaching. A specially organized history of practical doctrine and its formulations is of use only in the special science of Christian moral doctrine.

#195

Christianity's doctrine becomes real in the church's life, a life which is religious. Doctrine which has been realized in life is *ethics*; the means by which religious doctrine is realized in life is *worship*. The church's life thus has two aspects, an inner and an outer one. As the latter is conditioned by the former, it possesses its religious and

Christian character only from the former; otherwise, ethics would have to be seen as the product of other maxims. Thus the internal history of Christianity, as it shifts its attention from doctrine to life, has to investigate and explain the development and formation of Christian worship and Christian ethics.

#196

It is important to grasp the general manner in which the development and formation of doctrine takes place, namely, through the internal action of the Christian principle under the stimulation of external factors (##190–191). But this difference must be noted: doctrine is subject to the influence of ways of thinking, life to the influence of ways of acting. As doctrine is modified in accord with the kinds of images which happen to be generally prevalent at various times, so life is modified in accord with the practical maxims and external circumstances of human society which happen to be prevalent at various times. This directly impacts on ethics. But aesthetic sensitivity and activity influence worship insofar as it is necessarily involved with sensual forms. Both influences must be studied and clarified.

#197

In these studies, too, the distinction is to be drawn between what has grown up in the church's life purely from within the spirit of Christianity and as a result of its legitimate development and what is to be regarded merely as the effect of its outward life within society and its circumstances and so must be excluded from the church. How the church has done this and how it has tried to preserve Christian religious life in ethics and worship must be demonstrated by that history which is called as a result *history of Christian church discipline*. (Cf. #193.)

#198

The Christian church can exist only by possessing a definite polity. In part it had such a polity from its beginning, and in part it acquired it in the course of time. The church's polity embraces those arrangements in the institution's organic body by which it certifies the legitimate development of its doctrine and life within and by the same token resists those opposing factors without. Here opposing factors do not mean the world's opinions, maxims, tastes, and culture (##192,

196, 197), for these do not act as opponents but stimuli, at the worst only alien stimuli. Rather, the phrase refers to the state as the total society which extends its power even over the church as special kind of society (i.e., pursuing its special ends) but still existing within the state's territory and boundaries, and which by this extension *can* at least hinder the church's ends.

#199

The church's polity can thus be viewed once again as an internal structure through which the church is organized for the sake of its own ends—and an external one through which it seeks to establish and maintain its proper relation to the state—without prejudice to its ends. The history of the Christian church's polity can and should be seen in this double perspective.

> * This is not to say that in the historical study of the church's polity each of these divisions is treated separately but only that one must be distinguished from the other. Moreover, for certain purposes and studies, it might be good actually to separate them from one another.

#200

Under the history of the church's internal structure comes the entire development of the ecclesiastical organism in its various aspects. It too must be treated according to the general principle (##190, 191). Under the heading of external influences we must first of all note here the special destiny of Christianity to spread out to all the nations, the many requirements which have arisen from this, and the political and social forms adopted in various states. This constant attention to the church's well-being and to its goals, which are ever the same, will render perfectly clear to the student of history how the greatest and most significant changes in the domain of the church's history occur and must occur, since the church's whole polity, although in its main features necessary, is yet always merely a means to an end and so must always be formally structured in accord with the demands of that end.

> * The variety and multiplicity of the branches of the ecclesial organism are also the reason for distinguishing a general history from various special histories.

#201

The history of the church's external polity illustrates its position in every age vis-à-vis the state or states in whose domain it exists. From the perspective of legal theory, this position can only be understood as the result of a free and equable compromise. But historically it may be and often has in fact been at one time a situation of oppression of the church by the state, at another the dominion of the church over the state. But wherever one or the other unbalanced position has been the case, it must be regarded as the result of misunderstanding or mischance. It is not inherent in the principle of either the church or the state.

> * Since the church is both one and spread throughout all states and yet every state has its own peculiar character, the church's non-essential relations with one state will be different from those with another, i.e., there are in these cases clearly special histories. Furthermore, it is obvious that the only issues of church-state relations which can be included in church *history* are those which have ceased to be the case and have thus become part of the past. Those relations still existing and prevailing belong to another division of the science.

B.3. Sources of Church History

#202

Like any history, church history must fashion its material from the testimony of reliable witnesses. Just as its origin, Christianity's further course has, in addition to the sources of *general* history, its own special sources which have been handed down through all the centuries and which are called *ecclesiastical literature* (or ecclesiastical authorities). Historical theology and its rigorous study depend on knowledge, criticism, and employment of this, just as the study of biblical history and theology depend on knowledge, criticism, and employment of biblical literature. (Cf. ##124–128.)

> * Among these ecclesiastical writings, those which actually count as sources for church history because they deal with matters of their own time are to be distinguished from those other works of church history which present the history of the church of a past age even though from the original sources. These latter take their value from their sources

and the reliable use which their authors have made of those sources. In many cases, however, they have to substitute for the original sources, since so many of these have been lost.

#203

Sources, i.e., witnesses for the history of the church, fall into two classes. There are first of all those sources which can properly be regarded as such, in which the church itself speaks and gives testimony as to its doctrine, its discipline, and its polity in a particular age, in short, official public documents of the church. —Among these belong above all others the *decisions and decrees of great and universal councils of the church* in which the church speaks through its legitimate representatives. The decisions and decrees of so-called "local councils," which must be regarded as the immediate authentic statements of larger or smaller regions of the church, possess an authority no less great but mediated through the consensus of other regions or of the church at large. Lastly, according to the principles of the Catholic church, this also holds true of encyclical letters by individuals, especially by the chief members of the hierarchy or of noted church teachers whose statements the church acknowledges as its own because of their official position or their extraordinary spiritual gifts.

  * All these documents contain statements for the most part on Christian doctrine, seldom on ethics, still less on worship.

#204

The most important sources for the history of doctrine are especially the *creeds as public professions of faith*, both those established by councils and those accepted long before. They surpass all other witnesses to doctrine from the point of view of historical reliability. With regard to their meaning, however, they must often be explicated with the aid of other documents, especially the acts of the councils insofar as these are available.

  * The creeds of individual churches as well as those of separated sects are used in the same way as the doctrines of these communities.

#205

The way creeds function in the history of doctrine, *liturgies*, as ecclesial rules affecting the external direction and forms of official divine service, function in the history of worship. But since the forms of worship necessarily indicate the nature of worship and that nature includes the mysteries of faith, liturgies are also important for the history of doctrine.

* There are no universal liturgies as there are universal creeds.

#206

The other class of ecclesiastical literature is made up of writings which originate from private persons within the church and contain either their views on Christianity and the Christian church in all its aspects or historical reports and information on these subjects from their own or earlier times. These are the writings of the so-called *Fathers* and *Doctors of the church* as well as of learned persons generally in the church. Thus these are *private sources for the church*.

* The number of such writings and authors is naturally very large, although many, especially those from the earliest periods of the Christian church, have been lost. Consequently, the study of church history from its sources is the widest-ranging of all theological studies.

#207

To compose the whole of the church's history or even some part of it from these sources requires the same knowledge and skills as all historical work does. Just as exegesis has been elaborated for the explication of earliest Christianity from the Bible, so a similar theological discipline has been elaborated for explicating church history from its sources, a discipline which has two divisions, following the distinction between ecclesial sources referred to in ##203 and 206: so-called *synodics* and *patrology*. The first teaches the necessary knowledge and appropriate skills for understanding and interpreting the church's official sources, the second those for the private sources.

#208

The same subordinate tasks which are found in biblical exegesis are also found in synodics and patrology. Both have to verify the history of their sources in order to determine their authenticity with the help of criticism appropriate to these sources, and to ascertain from the particular styles of these sources their authors' meanings with the help of a hermeneutic which is rooted in the genius of those styles and those authors. Cf. ##126, 127.

* That biblical exegesis, which is *intrinsically* of no higher dignity than synodics and patrology, has enjoyed much more diligent and careful treatment than these is due simply to belief in the higher authority of the Bible's contents as sacred scripture, the word of God. Where this belief is absent, what has been until now the chief inducement for exegetical study must decline and share the same lot as the two aforementioned historical studies. That to this point synodics and patrology still lag so far behind exegesis is—even allowing for the difference between sacred scripture and ecclesiastical literature—a drawback which theology has to overcome.

#209

In the case of the history of ecclesiastical sources that inquiry is, of course, omitted which in biblical exegesis we called the history of the canon (##134, 135). For there is no canon of ecclesiastical literature in that same sense. Yet the pronouncements of general councils also possess their own kind of canonicity, to wit, that of creedal documents, through which they form a unique collection with special authority. And so at this point we must introduce the study of what council made which pronouncements and how and why it came to that decision. —All other lines of inquiry which pertain to the history of ecclesiastical literature, as that concerning their origins and what occasioned them, that about the authors and their personalities, about what they experienced, etc., and so especially about their authenticity and integrity, apply just as they do in biblical exegesis. For on a correct account of the history of these sources depend first of all how they are to be used and often even how they are to be understood.

#210

Criticism is, therefore, as indispensable in the study of these sources as it is in the study of the Bible, and for the same reasons. The principles and methods are also the same in the one case as in the other. But in this case the going is easier because the much greater richness of historical data provides more external grounds for one's conclusions and the fact that the kinds of images and styles of writing of church authors are much closer to our own provides more internal grounds.

* Nevertheless, criticism in church history has still not dealt thoroughly with the authenticity of many ecclesiastical writings.

#211

It is self-evident that linguistic studies are necessary for understanding ecclesiastical writers. Of course, here one has the advantage that almost all the church's primary sources were written in the two languages which any scholar is expected to know. Still there are many writings and documents important for church history written in oriental languages which someone would be required to know who intends to cast light on the history of the church from this quarter. And the language of other documents is not really or only seldom the classical tongue of Greece or Rome; it is a special dialect which is partly the product of the general decline of the classical languages and partly the peculiar speech of a particular province or of a certain author and often demands its own study.

* Partially as a result of the decline of the ancient languages and partially as a result of the doctrinal studies of the Doctors of the Christian church, there appeared a great number of new words and a way of writing which goes by the name *church style*.

#212

There is likewise a hermeneutic for sources for church history. Beyond the general principles of the art of interpretation (#156ff.) which have to be specially applied, there are other rules as well. The special requirement for correctly interpreting the Fathers of the church is knowledge of the historical facts about their personalities and their writings; for the correct interpretation of church documents there is special need for knowledge of ecclesiastical language. In actually using citations from the church Fathers, especially for the history of church doctrine, distinctions must be drawn between what may be simply culturally conditioned ways of expression and the actual meaning and between what may be merely the author's personal opinion and what he states as the universally accepted teaching of the church.

#213

It is already clear from what has been said in #202 that the history of the Christian religion and of the church has still other sources in addition to those mentioned to this point. Beyond general historical works, there are also other scientific and scholarly works, because, as has been stated, all scientific and cultural factors have influenced the development of doctrine, ethics, and worship, just as all the historical factors of society have influenced the church's polity. These influential factors are most reliably evidenced both in general historical works of past centuries and in their scientific works. The external history of Christianity must still have recourse to ancient histories and chronicles in order to fill out many of its gaps.

> * It need scarcely be recalled that, beyond knowledge of their own proper sources, church historians absolutely require the studies auxiliary to all history—archeology (*antiquitates ecclesiasticae*), geography, chronology, etc. Cf. #149ff. Their particular uses are easily seen.

B.4. Study and Method of Historical Theology

#214

Given the almost limitless scope of this part of the science, it seems necessary above all to establish definite principles for its study. Since history is a unity made up of infinite particulars, the one studying it cannot *begin* by sorting through these particulars and putting the unity together from them. Rather, he must start out by trying to obtain for himself as accurate an image of the unified whole as possible in order later to arrange and depict the individual features within it. To this end lectures and written works on church history will serve. As far as books are concerned, it is preferable to make use of those covering only one or a few periods in the church's history but which present it or them in greater detail rather than those which cover the whole history (we are not speaking of compendia at this point). The reason for this is not only to avoid the narrowness of view which virtually no historical writer escapes but also because it must be presumed that—all things being equal—writers of such histories have made better use of their sources, given the greater concentration of their work, and that is the key issue. And, in fact, books of this sort are also more numerous and more thorough than those which deal with the whole of church history. From these, then, one tries to sketch out for oneself an initial preliminary picture of the whole Christian era and Christian world.

#215

Anyone who feels called to surpass these limits and engage his own abilities in original inquiry and explanation must choose for himself some special branch of church history, for many are still very sketchy, indeed many are as good as unnoticed. Or if he prefers to engage in all branches, he selects one period and not too long a one. Either one course or the other is necessary because no one, even in the course of a whole lifetime, can study all aspects of Christian history from the sources. And so the energy of even the most gifted person must be limited to a particular task; else the historian will be obliged to rely on the prior work of others.

#216

Since this last alternative is both intrinsically less advisable and distasteful to able minds, it will receive short notice here. It finally comes down to the fact that no history possesses trustworthiness which is not the product of carefully examined and thoroughly understood sources, which can be said of only a very few works of church history. Most even well-known sources used from time immemorial—the writings of the Fathers of the church—are inadequate at present and not treated in accord with the demands of current criticism and interpretation. Among Protestants biblical studies have retarded the study of church history; among Catholics great and highly valued efforts in the field have been more concerned with collecting hitherto unknown sources and the means needed for their use than with examining and sifting those sources which are available. For criticism and correct understanding there is still an unbelievable amount to do. And this is the second principal reason why anyone who wants to do something useful in church history must limit himself to one particular branch or one particular period: first he will have to examine the sources.

#217

Whoever intends to undertake such work can do at least a little preparation for it even during his student years. Then his view must be always directed toward the whole of church history. Even at that point he may choose that branch of the whole study in which he will work, may familiarize himself with the literature and the tools, and what is even more important for the church historian, guard himself against prejudices which have previously (and to the present moment) bedeviled the study of church history and introduced all sorts of false notions into it. The same spirit which we described as of utmost and supreme import in the pursuit of biblical history and theology has the same import in historical theology. Of course, this can not and will not keep the inquirer from error about the nature of particular facts and phenomena, but it will allow him to discover the unifying center at which all the manifold phenomena, in what to the external view are their manifold contradictions, come together. Whoever has understood the spirit of Christianity in its original manifestation will constantly rediscover it later in its development and will know how to tie the two ends together into a unity. This it is which each one must learn early on and which is part of the circle of academic studies.

#218

The other rules for the method of study of church history are the same as those for the study of general history. There has already been discussion in #175ff. and in the foregoing sections of the spirit in which the whole history of Christianity should be examined. In considering and connecting individual facts, in this case as always in history, only the usual historical mode of construction can be followed which distinguishes the content of the fact and the observable changes it undergoes from the forces which cause them. This is the primary difference between genuine history and mere chronicle. — Historical construction employed on a mass of data to make clear their common orientation among divergently acting causes makes history pragmatic. It is readily apparent that the treatment of history must be pragmatic. It is simply arbitrary to fabricate some totally different practical orientation. The undeniably practical character of Christian church history is noted in #175—its ultimate pragmatism in #29.

> * Most of the straightforwardly historical sources for the history of Christianity in antiquity and the Middle Ages are simply chronicles in their form, but despite this, they are indispensable and of the greatest usefulness to actual history. Since in their explanation of data they interject no practical orientation whatsoever or, if occasionally they do, they in no way disguise it, they facilitate the discovery of the true practical orientation.

#219

The difference between general church history and various special histories has been mentioned already when treating of the major subjects of this history. Still more important for the study and presentation of history are the divisions which must be drawn between periods and what happened in them. In the internal development of any historical reality there must occur *turning points* when the development takes a new turn, new features emerge suddenly or powerfully, the previous flow of events is checked, and a new era is introduced. These moments of division (epochs) also exist in church history. Always following upon then are *eras* in which the changed circumstances which have been introduced extend their influence in all areas until they have completed their quiet transformation of everything; these are periods within church history. It follows naturally that one's first overview of all the phenomena and the way one divides the material of history depend on keen observation of these moments.

* In general church history epochs are easily discerned and make themselves quite clear; by contrast, periods lose in clarity because of the immense number of particulars. In the special branches, on the other hand, periods are more easily and obviously seen but epochs are not, unless recourse is had to general church history. For epochs are times of general change and activity in the Christian mind-set which affect all the elements of the church and produce in all of them a change which, if not of the same depth, is at least of the same character. So, for example, there cannot be an epoch which is formative in the church's doctrine which does not also affect ethics, worship, polity, etc., which is why at such moments the special history of one of these elements can only be understood in the light of general church history. But when each element is deeply affected by the mind-set of the epoch, then its development can proceed more freely and autonomously. This image of history is then once again that of one life and one action broken up into many particularities.

#220

How far one must devote attention to the whole of church history, apart from one's inclination and opportunity, comes down to the questions of how important certain issues in the church are for certain of the needs of the church and of what active role one plays in the church. For all the theologian's knowledge and labor are in behalf of the church and its well-being. The minimum knowledge which is needed by anyone at any time and in any role is given in #214. But various circumstances in which the church can find itself and the importance which particular branches of church history may then acquire may demand a deeper and broader knowledge of those particular branches on the part of those who wish to act for the church's good. To be educated, then, becomes a kind of duty. This holds for everyone in his special sphere of activity; each must decide for himself what the relation is between that sphere and knowledge of special branches of church history.

> * Since no one can work for the church at large or within a particular community without some knowledge of its present situation, the absolute need for the study of church history thus becomes clear, and for the study of modern even more than ancient church history. For the present situation of the church is only the result of previous moments in history, and most directly of the most recent. Whatever is now deplorable within the church has become so only because genuinely Christian principles have ceased to have any effect or destructive principles have intruded themselves. Each person can discover accordingly what work is cut out for him.

II. Scientific Theology

A. Foundational Studies

#221

The distinction between foundational studies and the fully elaborated system of the science is based on the reasons given in #72. Those reasons come together in the more important distinction between what may be called the *essence* of Christianity and what may be taken as the realized form of this essence, at least as this has been available to us to this point. The scientific examination of the essence is the task of foundational studies; the scientific study of the form of this essence as it has existed until now is the task of the system of specialized theology.

#222

As is the case with Christianity generally, its essence can be regarded and studied either as a pure concept (or a system of concepts) or as a vital force which reshapes the world. Or, following the previously formulated distinction between Christianity as a religious system considered in the abstract and a religious system manifested in life, the question can be put: What is the essence of the system of the Christian religion, and what is the essence of the Christian church? Foundational studies are divided up in the same way as specialized science and the historical study of Christianity.

#223

By the very nature of the case, it is impossible to ask the question, What can be known as posited which has not yet been posited? So, examination of Christianity in foundational studies presupposes historical knowledge of it. But the essence of a thing is not yielded in *mere* historical or empirical knowledge of it. First of all, the concept of an essence is a purely rational concept; the essence of some particular thing can only be discovered through its examination by reason, which isolates in the thing as posited precisely those characteristics or qualities which constitute the thing essentially. Since such examination is done through reason and according to its principles, it is always scientific and philosophical in the accepted meaning of the word.

#224

So we must first explain how the essence of the Christian religion can be discovered in the manner just described, and what procedures establish it. At the outset, Christianity is posited in the process of abstraction as one unified whole, at least as one sum of religious doctrines. If this sum is a unified whole and that whole a system (which question has an immediate importance for reason), then it must be characterized by fundamental doctrines, i.e., by doctrines which stand out most strongly in the historical view of Christianity. But the essence of the Christian religion is not known only from the content of its fundamental doctrines but also from the manner of its origin. At least since it itself regards its particular manner of origin as intrinsic to its essence, this must be examined in foundational studies.

#225

What has been said to this point applies equally to the Christian church. Precisely because it is the living embodiment of the ideas of Christianity, both their product and their channel, there has to be some essential quality in it. This is the essence of its inward meaning. Furthermore, as a definite and positive institution it must bear within it some essential quality—in terms of its origin, its orientation, and its end—which it cannot efface without altering its nature and destroying itself. This is its historical essence.

#226

These ways of inquiring into the essence of the Christian religion and the church make their appearance as soon as human understanding is no longer satisfied with the simple historical interpretation of Christianity and instead seeks unity within the multitude of ideas and data, i.e., they appear as soon as the need is felt for a scientific knowledge of Christianity. In any case this must occur whenever the scientific mind awakens in the realm of human knowledge and draws into its orbit every subject of interest to reason. Then the theologian feels that need on the one hand and on the other is led by his commitment to Christianity to assert its claims before the court of reason and is forced to render an account of Christianity. This is to be an account of Christianity by the standards of reason. In this undertaking foundational studies already take the form of *apologetics*.

#227

Moreover, as a specific form of religion, Christianity stands in opposition both temporally and essentially to other equally specific forms of religion. In this opposition the essence of each religion takes on form, and the Christian religion must then justify not only its essence but its form as contrasted with other forms, since each religion makes the same sorts of claims for itself. As a truly scientific first-line defense, it is forced to compare its essence and its manner of inception with those of the religions with which it is contrasted. And so, after Christian apologetics, there appears a polemics whose goal is to demonstrate that the form of the Christian religion is alone valid rationally (relatively speaking).

    *   Polemics is really only apologetics under the incentive of opposition.

#228

As the Christian religion stands in opposition to other forms of religion (both prior to it and contemporary with it), so different ecclesiastical factions are opposed to one another in the history of Christianity. In this way the essence of the church also takes form, or rather forms, and each form of church tries to justify itself in contrast to the others before the court of reason. This justification is offered on the basis of the essence of its inward meaning and on that of the historical essence of its inception. Each faction's goal must be to prove that it corresponds to the inward meaning and the outward origin of the primitive Christian church. It can readily be seen, however, that the latter task is impossible for any church which has arisen later on.

> * There is no comparison between the Christian churches taken as a whole and non-Christian ones, because the very idea of a church is exclusively Christian. In Christianity alone is religion simply open to humanity without any connection to nationality or citizenship; thus, the church is free and independent. The religions of the ancient world were thoroughly national, and so the state was itself the church. Mosaic religion was no less national, the union of its members forming a church-state in accord with the theocratic principle of its origin and not a church at all; as a result of the weaknesses of sacerdotal government the church-state became a state-church.

#229

The foundational study preparatory to scientific theology is thus as regards its intellectual form a *philosophical construction* of the essence of Christianity. As regards its orientation it is *apologetic theology* in which what is usually called *apologetics* can be distinguished from *polemics*. And both these secondary divisions include examinations of the *system of religion* and of the *church*.

A.1. Apologetics

#230

Exposition of the essence of the system of Christian religion is the primary task of apologetics—as a foundational study for scientific theology. Without knowledge of its essence no authentic knowledge or science of Christianity is possible. From the ideal perspective, systematically considered, the essence is found through the basic doctrines of Christianity (#224); these are found through a universal perspective which undergirds them, seeing and comprehending everything from a religious point of view. This perspective can therefore be called the *root idea*, the comprehensive idea of Christianity. For this to be discoverable, it must be openly asserted in historical Christianity or at least contained in its basic doctrines. The first concern of Christian apologetics is to uncover this root idea, to give it historical and then philosophical form, and finally to evaluate it. Then the basic doctrines must be constructed from it and examined individually and collectively in light of the root idea. In this way knowledge is gained of both the essence of the Christian system and its internal coherence, and the *inner truth of the Christian religion* is demonstrated.

> * The principles with whose assistance this inquiry is carried on are naturally first and foremost the universal principles of reason in the domains of religion and morality. If, however, one looks historically at the development of these principles to their present form, it will be found that they are largely abstracted from Christianity, and thus Christianity is really its own demonstration.

#231

While the inner essence of Christianity is sought, its outward or historical essence must also be sought and demonstrated. This is found through the manner of its growth and preservation. As to its growth, i.e., its *origin*, a religious system can be either created or given. But the concept of being given leads directly to the concept of revelation, and as Christianity has very definitely claimed to be revealed, initial inquiry into its historical essence is inquiry into its revealed character. This inquiry can only be conducted by means of general principles concerning universal revelation—i.e., concerning the relation of God to the natural world and to the human spirit, the way supernatural realities can be known, and the manner in which reason can deal with them. There thus is a theory and critique of all revelation by which Christianity is tested. The demonstration achieved in this way is the demonstration of the *positive divine quality of Christianity*, which is a quite different matter from the truth of its doctrines.

#232

Beyond its immediate beginnings, the way in which Christianity has maintained its identity at the same time as it has been communicated to the world is also part of its historical essence. It was communicated through oral preaching and through scripture. (Its creedal tradition is secondary to these two.) Even if one accepts that the Christian religion originated through an initial revelation, when the word of God had been proclaimed *once and for all* one can imagine it either as having been left to its fate or as being maintained by the same Spirit by whom it was introduced and proclaimed. As can readily be seen, it is not a matter of indifference for the historical essence of Christianity and for faith in revelation which of these alternatives is taken as true. There is thus this third line of inquiry in Christian apologetics: has Christianity, which is positive and divine in its origin, maintained this character in its tradition? The demonstration which leads one to answer "yes" is the demonstration of the *divine character of Christianity's means of tradition* and of their importance.

> * Most theologians call this the proof for the inspiration of sacred scripture. But this is entirely beside the point in our concern here. For scripture is neither the only, nor the earliest, nor the ordinary tradition of the originating Christian revelation. If the tradition of that revelation to the world is to be protected, then it must be protected first of all and especially in its most usual means. Otherwise, of what use would the inspiration of the sacred authors have been to subsequent ages? If we are to be consistent in our belief that the word of God is still to be found in their writings, then we must regard what we term their inspiration as something which perdures, certainly not in them and not even in their writings, but in the whole institution of Christianity.

#233

The same three tasks in which the apologetics—*demonstratio*—of the Christian religion consists recur in the apologetics of the Christian church. Just as all the individual doctrines of Christianity are connected to certain basic doctrines and these are joined together in one root idea, so all the phenomena of the church are connected to certain basic forms and these spring from the idea of the church. So the apologetics of the Christian church must first form its idea out of the root idea of the Christian religion, i.e., it has to show how it is manifested in living externalized phenomena. This coincidence between the church and Christianity as a system of religion is the reason why it is the Christian church. From the idea of the church in which its orientation or its ultimate end is immediately posited, its basic forms, the essential marks of its inner spirit, and the essential phenomena of its outward life must be constructed. This is the church's inner reality: the coincidence of the concrete church with its *idea* through which it becomes the *true church*.

#234

Inquiry into the church's historical essence follows the pattern of inquiry into its inner essence. As with Christianity, the inquiry deals with the church's origin and with its continuance. As a union of persons for religious ends, a church can be formed at its start (and so gradually spread) either by a coming together motivated simply by choice, and so accidentally, or as a result of a higher call entailing moral obligation, and so necessarily. The binding authority of a church depends on such a call entailing obligation. Only in that way does it possess binding authority and, without it, has none. But a church's authority, like its call, can come either from human beings or from God. In the first case, it is a human institution, a kind of state-church; in the other case, it is the church of God. All this must now be applied to the historical Christian church and inquiry must be made as to whether in its essence it is accidental or necessary, and in the latter case (for in the former case there would be nothing essential in the historical church) whether it has been founded under human or divine authority. Thus apologetics of the church has to demonstrate that the *church of Christ is in its origins a divine institution*.

> * There can be no such thing as a human church in the strict sense. For any call entailing moral obligation which can arise in a social setting or which can exist between person and person for some social end is already contained in the idea of the state. The church would then dissolve into the state. Cf. #228.

#235

As can be seen, the working out of this demonstration depends first of all on a presupposition which must be established in the apologetics of religion, that of the divinity of Christianity as a whole and of the divine character of Christ in particular. In fact, through this presupposition the demonstration to be given at this point becomes possible. It can be and actually is worked out in a historical manner by confirming the data which constitute the above-mentioned claim on Christ's part which entails moral obligations for all people. And this claim is made either immediately through Christ's own clear statement or mediately through the means which he established to make his will known. The relevant data must be drawn from the whole history of that earliest period.

#236

If the Christian church possesses the positive character of divinity in view of the authority given it just as the Christian religion possesses it in view of its origin, then the question once again arises for the former as it did for the latter: how has it preserved its original character? For, viewed in itself, the originating fact of revelation and of the establishment of the church involves personal and temporary gifts which do not by themselves guarantee the doctrine that is revealed and the religious community that is founded against subsequent distortion and deviation from their goals. Thus, with regard to the church also inquiry must be made whether and by what means it preserves its original Christian character. This is the notion of *the infallibility of the church*, which, as can be readily seen, is the same as that of its indestructibility or certainly agrees with it. Working out the proof of this infallibility and of the church's authority, which is dependent upon it, is the third task of ecclesiastical apologetics.

* Obviously it is one and the same principle by which the original character of Christian revelation and of the church is preserved, just as it is one and the same from which it sprang.

A.2. Polemics

#237

Polemics is distinguished from apologetics neither in its orientation, for in both the objective is justification of Christianity and of the institutionalized church, nor in its principles and technique, for in both the principles are general ideas on religion and the institutionalized church in which the positive ideas of the Christian religion and the Christian church are included so as to show their coincidence in both instances. So it is distinguished from apologetics only by the fact that apologetics recognizes no contradiction save that of the natural and positive but overcomes this in the idea, whereas in polemics a positive reality stands in contradiction to a positive reality, and this contradiction is significant not only for the phenomenon but also for the idea.

> * Polemics thus presumes that in terms of general ideas there is a difference among existing forms of religion and church and that one is not as good as the other. In other words, from the standpoint of indifferentism all polemics is impossible or at least irrational; and so, in recent times, its importance has obviously declined.

#238

Since there are many existing forms of positive religion standing in opposition to Christianity, their scientific polemics take many different forms. And it is natural that every other form of religion, if it has developed a real theology, has shaped its polemic in opposition to Christianity. Likewise, since there are many different ecclesiastical sects in conflict within the sphere of Christianity, their polemics are directed against one another. Since polemics finds its immediate origins in the importance which the theologian attaches to his religion and his church and the concern he experiences when others fail to recognize them, and since that importance and concern disappear when the discussion is of an extinct religion and a defunct church, polemics can only be concerned with currently existing ones.

> * There can be no true polemics directed against indifferentism which denies anything positive in religion and church, still less against unbelief which denies religion and church completely. Both would first have to be led by basic apologetics to the recognition of universal ideas and universal positive realities.

#239

Since there can be no argument about truth except on the basis of generally acknowledged principles from which the argument can proceed, the first task of polemics is to establish such generally acknowledged premises. In terms of the polemics of the Christian religion, these premises are universal ideas on religion and universally recognized facts having to do with the history of Christianity. In terms of ecclesiastical polemics they are Christian ideas and facts which are recognized by all parties.

#240

A person can miss the truth either by departing from it or falling short of it; the first is error in its immediate sense, and the second leads to it. Error is a movement beyond the limits of truth; it sets its own limits and acts in divergence from the truth. Falling short of the truth is sloth, a result of flagging energy in the on-going development of (religious) principles. In this way it is truncated. In one of these two ways the point is reached where the imperfect—the part—is mistaken for the perfect—the whole.

#241

This foundation provides both the criteria and the mode of procedure for polemics in response to religions opposing Christianity and to Christian sects opposing the original institutionalized church. It provides the criteria because error can only be exposed by showing that it is a distortion or an inadequacy; it provides the mode of procedure because polemics directed against a given opponent demonstrates how one or the other is the case.

#242

Applying this to polemics directed against religions opposed to Christianity, we note first that at its beginning earlier polemics stood in living opposition to polytheism and the mythology of the ancient world which now has only a historical importance. But polytheism can only be understood as the distortion of an idea into an image, or of inner feeling into sensuousness. That is how the earliest heralds and defenders of Christianity treated it in their polemics. And that debasement has proven very productive.

* Likewise, the other pagan religions which began at some ancient and, in most cases, uncertain time and which are still in existence are at their origins distorted and in their later forms inadequate.

#243

Since the dawn of Christianity the Mosaic religion seems (and seemed even before it) to be obviously inadequate to the very idea in which it was conceived. Mohammedanism as well, which is, aside from Christianity, the most widespread religion at present, can be understood only as an inadequate version of the spirit and culture of Christianity. Wherever it has been established, it has had to struggle to work itself out of some very impoverished notions of religion even to reach that level of somewhat better ideas which is typical of it, and wherever it has succeeded in supplanting Christianity, the latter must never have been truly and properly rooted.

#244

There must be a perspective from which distortion with its divergent tendencies and inadequacy with its power of persistence (*vis inertia*) can be grasped as necessary phenomena in the history of the development of religious ideas. But this cannot become the concern of Christian polemics, which is entirely confined to the realm of Christianity as one particular religion and which would cease to exist were that perspective adopted. Such a perspective is indeed implied in the root idea of Christianity; the Bible often refers to it but calls it a mystery hidden in the depths of the divine wisdom.

#245

The various ecclesiastical sects which have appeared in the Christian sphere in opposition to the Catholic church must be regarded in this church's polemics as either distorted or inadequate. Since the most ancient sects have largely disappeared or are at least no longer significant, they now have only historical importance, and Catholic polemics is confined to the two great schisms which still exist in the east and the west. That in the east seems obviously an inadequacy, that in the west no less obviously a headstrong distortion.

> * As these different sects must also have their own polemics, from their perspective their principles can only be justified by attempting to demonstrate corruption in the present development of the Christian principle. Consequently, Catholic polemics has to provide defense against this attack.

#246

Distortion, inadequacy, or corruption can occur either in one element of the common life of the church or in several or in all. In doctrine, this would be *heresy*, in worship and lifestyle, *separatism*, and in the church's polity and government, *schism*. And it is the proper and final task of any polemics conclusively to convict any given sect of one or the other or all three: heresy as regards the creed, separatism as regards liturgy and discipline, schism as regards the organic unity of Christianity.

> * By the nature of the case, heresy, separatism, and schism are usually related to one another.

#247

There is a perspective within which distortion of or inadequacy to the idea of Christianity, and thus heresy, separatism, and schism, are understood to be necessary phenomena in the history of the development of Christian ideas and the life of the Christian church. When this is based on the claim that no historical phenomenon can ever correspond precisely to its idea and consequently the various ecclesiastical doctrines and communions are just many attempts to express Christianity's unrealizable idea and unrealizable church in a concrete but always imperfect fashion, then this perspective is *ecclesiastical indifferentism*. It can possess no significance for polemics because it negates all polemics. But when it is based on the claim that every temporal form calls forth its antithesis and only attains its definite character through that antithesis, then this is the very perspective from which the Catholic church has always viewed all schisms and sects within the Christian sphere and has decided that, although they are divorced from that sphere, they belong to it when it is considered as an entirety. Once polemics has attained this perspective, its task is finished.

B. Specialized Science

#248

Under specialized science belongs the study of the evolution of the whole of Christianity to the present day from its essence (#221). As regards its contents, it is thus an expansion of foundational studies; as regards its principle, it deals with tracing all particular phenomena to their root or with establishing their truth. It goes without saying that it is complete and so must encompass all particular phenomena which have appeared in the development of Christianity.

#249

As science in the strict sense, it deals entirely with ideas and regards whatever it treats as an idea and evaluates it as an idea, first in itself and then in relation to other ideas. This distinguishes it essentially from so-called historical theology, which confines itself primarily to the data as such and verifies them as data purely historically, i.e., tries to uncover their purely historical truth, unconcerned whether what is found to be historically true or historically determined is also genuinely Christian, has developed out of the idea of Christianity, and is in agreement with it and with all other Christian ideas.

#250

Since scientific theology presupposes historical theology in that it does not seek out the historical data of Christianity but must recast the already verified data as pure concepts and bind them into a scientific unity, its essential task is to compare each individual concept to the ideas and show its congruence with them and above all with that idea (key concept) which it is supposed to express and through it with the root idea of Christianity itself. Only in this way can the inner truth of the concept be found, and since this operation is repeated with each individual concept, the inner—non-historical—truth of the whole Christian system is demonstrated.

> * This is the procedure in scientific theology in consequence of its own self-notion and on the presupposition of a precise and objective historical theology. But since we do not possess such a historical theology, since indeed scarcely any attempts have been made toward a biblical theology, and since church history remains woefully imperfect and, even more seriously, the opinions of ecclesiastical sects have intruded even into the study of general history, scientific theology is forced to engage in preliminary historical work. And so until now it has been unable to exist in its *pure* form.

#251

In the course of that testing of particular concepts yielded by history against the idea (or ideas) of Christianity it cannot fail to happen that many which are historically true must be found which do not correspond to the Christian ideas to which they are supposed to correspond. Such a concept then appears as a malformation in Christianity's development; it must be reckoned as an error or mistake and be excluded from the system. So a kind of polemics—as an advanced form of that which in foundational studies deals with major and generally opposing positions—runs through the whole science, just as apologetics first attains its finished form in the fully elaborated science.

> * What we had previously to exclude from historical theology in #193* now rightfully finds its place in scientific theology. As much as dogmatism within history, the lack of a strictly scientific theology has led the historical theologian to trespass within the domain of the science.

#252

In its outward form scientific theology is brought to completion in the same way as every other science, namely when every individual concept is assigned to its place because only in that place can it be *understood*. To this end it is necessary, both by means of a thorough deduction of concepts from one another and from the idea at the root of the more general concepts and by means of relating these ideas to one another, to assign the place where each particular concept fits. Thus the whole treatment of the science becomes *systematic*.

#253

As regards their contents, the chief subjects are arranged in this scientific study as they were in historical study (#179). Scientific theology thus divides immediately into two main branches: *the system of Christian ideology* and *the system of the Christian church*. The first has to deal with Christian doctrine, the second with the structure of the Christian religious commonwealth rooted in that doctrine.

#254

The doctrine and ideas of Christianity may be viewed and so studied either under their theoretical or their practical aspects. They are presented under the first aspect in *dogmatics*, under the second in *moral theology*. The system of Christian ideology thus includes Christian dogmatics and Christian moral theology. In similar fashion, the Christian commonwealth or the church may be viewed under two aspects. As a living organism, it has an interior spiritual life and an exterior bodily form as the bearer of its interior life. The inner essence of the church is living religion undergirded by devotion and worship; the exterior bodily form is its polity. The system of the Christian church thus divides into the *theory of Christian worship* (this word standing for everything which has impact on practical religion) and the *theory of Christian church polity* (Pneumatology or somatology of the church).

> * It may easily be seen that the treatment of all branches of specialized science must be shaped from the perspective of each ecclesiastical sect and so differently in each one. At least, this is self-evident as regards the theory of the church and of worship. But if, as regards doctrine, there has always been greater divergence on the theoretical side, this can only be the result of the fact that the practical doctrine of Christianity has never been elaborated in all its ramifications like the dogmatic doctrine or that moral theology has remained independent of dogmatics. However advantageous this may appear from a practical perspective, from the standpoint of science it must always be seen as an imperfection in the system of moral theology.

B.1. System of Christian Doctrine

#255

The task of this branch of scientific theology is to study the doctrine of Christianity in the development which it has undergone up until now and in its relation to the Christian confession, whose tradition one shares, by constructing the whole from its idea with systematic coherence. Since this holds true in exactly the same way for both the purely theoretical and the practical sides of doctrine, what will be said below about this branch of theology holds true of both Christian moral theology and dogmatics without requiring any discussion of these two specializations separately—with the exception, of course, of a few comments which should be made on the study of Christian moral theology to this point.

#256

A unified system of ideas which is not to be thought of as the dead tradition of a bygone age but as the development of a living reality has within it two elements—a *fixed* and a *mutable* one. The first is that which has been *closed* by development up to now, the second that which is still *being understood* as it develops. Within Christian doctrine an idea which has been closed, because it is closed, is called *dogma*. If it is a purely speculative matter, it is called *dogma speculativum* or just *dogma*; if it is a practical matter, it is called *dogma practicum*, a practical rule of action, or a duty, etc.

#257

Either the idea has had this quality of finality from its inception, in which case it is posited *as such* (*dogma explicitum*), or it has been posited in and with other closed ideas but is not yet recognized in itself, at least not generally (*dogma implicitum*). This latter kind of idea can only achieve its finished state through further development within the church and it is the church which gives it that finished state (*dogma declaratum*). —The study of all these ideas and doctrines, whether speculative or practical, makes up the first part of Christian dogmatics and moral theology and is generally acknowledged as essential.

#258

Whatever in Christian doctrine is not yet closed is mutable. Since the quality of being closed is a criterion of Christian *truth* which is uniquely objective and important—to the church—and a mutable concept lacks this criterion, as a result, the latter is called *opinion*. And when disagreement on it still reigns among scholars within the church, it is called an *opinion of a school* or a *theological opinion*. Nevertheless, despite this lack of agreement, it can in fact be Christian truth which has simply not yet developed to the stage at which it can be acknowledged as such universally in the church. For this reason and because it is characteristic of Christian doctrine to unfold itself ever more clearly and the theologian as a teacher of his church is called to participate in this, opinions are not merely accidental but necessary subjects of investigation and study in dogmatics and moral theology.

#259

And in this we see the connection of science to Christian doctrine and to the church. Science gives ever-new stimulus to the development of Christian doctrine and leads its mutable elements toward their final forms. Hence it labors on the church's behalf, since the impetus toward further developments and more precise conceptual formulation can only come from individuals, and before the final form of an idea can be reached, science must prepare the way. This is the role of science in the formation of the church's doctrine.

> * On the basis of this role of science, decisions can be made as to how far what we have called opinions and are in fact stimuli toward further doctrinal development are to be admitted in the study of this science. Specifically, only that can be admitted from which such development may still be anticipated. Opinions which may indeed have had weight for a long time in the science but which have remained without effect on doctrine are to be regarded simply as testimony of a certain intellectual period and have their place at most in the history of the science but not in the science itself.

#260

The theologian and his scientific efforts are to be evaluated by the stance he takes with regard to doctrine. The effort to hold fast to what has been definitively closed in doctrine and to construe what is mutable in the sense of and in agreement with what has been closed is *orthodoxy*. The attempt to make what has been fixed mutable or to construe what is mutable in opposition to what is fixed is *heterodoxy*. Finally, whoever denies the mutability of doctrine either because he rejects the idea altogether or elevates opinion into dogma is called *hyperorthodox*.

> * Every position which is scientific and which therefore does not forget its positive character is necessarily orthodox. It can, however, very easily appear heterodox to those who are untrained in science and hyperothodox to those who are wary of everything positive.

#261

What is closed in Christian doctrine is historically given in its sources and the details belong to historical theology (at least insofar as they are historical). Scientific theology has only to trace what is closed to its idea and to formulate it in accord with that idea. But when something historically given—something positive—is elevated to the level of an idea, it carries with it all the ideas which were part of the scientific world in the age with which it was connected, and these ideas influence its scientific form. Hence, there is the phenomenon within the history of the science of Christian doctrine and the scientific study of individual doctrines that not only the mutable element of doctrine, which is perfectly understandable, but the definitively closed ideas of Christianity as well have little by little in all their forms been recast in the currently dominant philosophical systems.

> * Precisely this charge has been leveled against the scientific statement of Christian doctrine, that through such mixture with time-bound systems it has made itself dependent upon them and must become as changeable as they are. This charge would be well-founded if the doctrine of Christianity, devoid of its own ideas, had had to borrow them initially from some philosophy or other or had lost its positive character in its scientific statement. But since neither of these is the case, this charge can only rest on a misunderstanding. Due to the doggedly positive quality which Christian doctrine possesses, its essence must remain ever the same in any *particular* scientific style of presentation, and due to the peculiarly ideal quality which indwells it, its statement at any given time appears only as an accidental form of which many must be tried and of which many are found adaptable to the ideas of Christianity as naturally and readily as to any other ideas.

#262

As there are two elements within the Christian doctrinal system (##256–258), so there are also incomplete ways of presenting that system. Single-focused study of what is closed in doctrine is *symbolics*. It stands necessarily in close relation to particular forms of church—ecclesiastical sects—each of which possesses its own peculiar confession and so its own creed. In consequence, each sect compares its creed with those of others. Thus symbolics serves an ecclesial purpose. In a still narrower sense, although one derived from this same purpose, symbolics is also called the study of *doctrinal differences* among the various Christian confessions.

#263

Whether from the decline of ecclesiastical conflict which naturally leads to the symbolic treatment of Christian doctrine or on account of a prevalent hunger for speculation, the theological mind turns its attention to the mutable element in doctrine and increasingly busies itself with it; thus arises *scholasticism* or scholastic theology. Its immediate end is the further development of doctrine; its strength is its speculative spirit; its success depends on its constant recourse to what has been definitively closed and is for that very reason highly problematic. Genuine dogmatics is neither simple symbolics nor simple scholasticism but a combination of the two.

> * From what has been said, it can be understood why from the Middle Ages until the Reformation theology existed in the form of scholasticism, but since then, especially among Protestants, in the form of symbolics.

#264

What has been said to this point applies not only to Christian dogmatics but also to Christian moral theology, which, as the term is used here, is simply the study of the doctrine of the Christian religion in its practical dimensions but which remains always the study of one and the same doctrine as in dogmatics. Thus the ideas of Christianity remain the same *in themselves*, whether they are viewed in their purely speculative dimension as in dogmatics or in their practical-speculative dimension as in moral theology. The distinction between pure speculation and practical speculation consists in the fact that the first explores *what is*, whereas the second explores *how what is comes to be*. And so Christian moral theology is in fact not *applied* [angewandte] dogmatics but *reverse* [umgewandte] dogmatics. Both are applied but in actual life, not in a body of knowledge.

> * It may be sufficient to demonstrate the unity and difference of these two theological disciplines in their key ideas. Christianity's fundamental religious insight and thus the root idea of Christian theology is the idea of the Kingdom of God as a moral order of the world. If this is looked at as it exists in itself and as it is established by God, then it appears as the culmination of the decrees of eternal providence made manifest in time. To explain this on the basis of its idea is the work of dogmatics. If this moral order of the world is looked at in the way it comes to be and is realized, it appears as the product of an all-encompassing and all-penetrating moral power which gathers and binds everything into unity. Such a power can only be holy love which radiates outward from the center of this unity, embraces every individual, and so realizes the moral order of the world. That love is the principle of Christian morality, and to explain all moral action on its basis is the

task of Christian ethics. Fall, restoration, and eternal life are seen as the key moments in the dogmatic development of the decrees of eternal providence. These same ideas are the cardinal points of Christian moral theology: the fall as the unhappy situation from which a moral theology has to begin, because no one is good save God alone and because what are to be united in love must initially be encountered as foreign to one another and mutually alienated; restoration as moral improvement in which all duties and the means to perform them become clear; eternal life as moral reward and the attainment of our final end.

#264a
[originally misnumbered 264 in the 1819 edition]

Thanks to the close relationship between the two disciplines, they could in an earlier age be treated as a single science and can still be so treated now. The separation of moral theology from dogmatics occurred in an age when the old scholasticism was abandoned and a new scientific approach to dogmatics had not yet been discovered, i.e., it occurred in an age when speculation, until then prevalent, had become remote from life and from ideas and fallen into decay, when science in the grip of a general revolution attracted systematic minds initially by its practical aspects because these were more readily apparent. Although these factors which would have to entail a separation of practical from purely speculative science in any age now no longer prevail, and although speculative science has been newly established and the relation between it and practical science is recognized, yet the tumultuous state of science and greater rigor in the study of the theoretical and practical doctrine of Christianity still render their separation not only advisable but necessary.

#265

But once this separation became established, it produced an unavoidable problem which even now Christian moral theology has not overcome, namely, that it has remained to this point more a philosophical than a Christian moral theory. In all the manuals, large and small, of Christian moral theology we find at the outset questions which may well belong in a rationalist moral theory but not in a Christian one. So, for example, there are general discussions of the moral nature of the human being, his capacities and powers, of freedom, the idea of the good, the principle of morality, etc. General observations on these topics ought to be presumed from philosophy, but by contrast, what should be presented is what is unique to the Christian vision, or better, those general observations should be presented in an authentically Christian form. The same is true in the theory of moral obligations. This is usually construed in accord with some arbitrary model and undergirded with biblical texts or with a higher sanction appended to these rational obligations by the authority of Christ. Instead, our obligations should be derived from the root idea of Christian doctrine from which the basic principle of its practical dimension can be deduced and, from this point of view, the standards of obligation construed in terms of our final end. One could not give the name "Christian dogmatics" to an arbitrary system (if any such could exist) rooted in metaphysics which borrows its doctrines of God from rational theology, its doctrines of the human person from anthropology and psychology, its doctrines of the universe at large from ontology and cosmology and furnishes the whole thing with biblical citations and biblical authority; just so, no moral theory constructed in the same fashion can be called authentically Christian. An authentically Christian moral theory can only arise through carefully drawing out the practical import of the speculative ideas of Christianity, in short, through taking dogmatics as its base.

> * Were it the goal of the study of Christian moral theology to show "how the whole of Jesus' religious doctrine in its necessary and fundamental concepts and in its ultimate tendency may be perfectly harmonized with the moral religion of reason," or, as it is unambiguously expressed, "that in its fundamental ideas and its final end Christianity is in fact nothing other than the religion of pure reason" (which is presumably more readily demonstrated from its practical aspect)—then such a demonstration would not be the work of Christian moral theology but of Christian philosophy of religion; and if the latter is to be treated in a true and authentic fashion, it would have to be done on the basis of its own resources. Besides, no reasonable estimate of Christian moral theory can deny either the fact of its positive origin or the equally indisputable fact of its uniqueness.

#266

As there are partial ways of studying Christian dogmatics because of their special ends (##262, 263), so too are there in Christian moral theology but for different reasons. In moral theology Christian doctrine is oriented toward and applied to life. But this has two aspects, an internal one dealing with *motives* and an external one dealing with *actions*. So, because moral theory should govern life, it has to determine motives in general and the form of action—i.e., law or duty—in particular. When one approach to Christian moral theology tends to give primary emphasis to Christian motivation, either because it regards external forms with indifference or because it believes that in action the right motive will spontaneously find its right form, then we have that moral theory which has long been known by the name *mystical* or more generally as *mystical* or *ascetical theology*.

> * It can easily be seen why mystical theology in its beginnings in the Middle Ages would appear antagonistic to scholasticism and will always prove to be so. Motivation stems from the free action of the heart, and any formalization by speculative concept or by practical rule confines that action, since it wishes to subordinate it to the form. Thus, mysticism hates conceptualization and formalization.

#267

On the other hand, when an approach to Christian moral theology emphasizes the definition of the external form of the act and especially the precise definition of law and obligation, then we have a moral theory which has also long been known under the name of *casuistry*, since many particular circumstances and situations (*casus*) must be subsumed under one fixed principle. Casuistry is to practical doctrine what scholasticism is to speculative doctrine and arises from the latter when it is directed more to ethical issues than to dogmatic ones.

> * Familiar casuistry has gotten a bad name more because of neglect of sound principles and acceptance of unsound ones than for any intrinsic reason. It certainly is part of the development of Christian doctrine in its practical dimensions that application of its practical maxims to life should take as much account of individual circumstances as possible. —Nevertheless, neither casuistry alone nor mysticism alone is a complete moral doctrine. A complete moral doctrine must incorporate both the one and the other within it: the spirit of mysticism so as not to miss the essence of Christian motivation because of aridly defined obligations, the flesh of casuistry so as not to surrender actions to vague and obscure emotions.

B.2. System of the Christian Church

#268

The basic notion of the Christian church is that it is a necessary development of Christian ideas into an objective phenomenon in a religious society of persons and that in this phenomenon Christianity's basic intuition—the Kingdom of God—attains empirical reality and objective meaning. —The basis of the Christian church, as of any ecclesial institution whatever, is doctrine, which, because it can bring about the unification of persons into one church, must necessarily be held in common—a common religious tradition. Apart from such common doctrine, it is as impossible for a religious society actually to come together, and when it has come together, to hold together as it is to imagine such a society without any religious ideas at all. Commonality of doctrine is thus the first condition for any ecclesial institution. A church *comes into being* through common doctrine; it is the *cornerstone* on which it is built and depends. And so discussion of it must precede discussion of the church.

> * For the same reason the first thing which a church must possess is its creed—its common religious tradition stated publicly and definitively.

#269

A church comes into being through a common religious tradition, but that is not the *end*, at least not the unique and final end, of a church once it has come into being. Its religious ideas, the subject and content of its tradition, are progressively realized in individuals and in a church as a whole. The religious tradition must be transformed into religious motivation, into religious life—in a word, into *piety*. Piety and all that pertains to it is the final end of a church. Everything that furthers piety, which is ordinarily summarized under the term *devotion*, is the means to the end. But piety as actually experienced depends first on the ideas which are present in a church, ideas whose realization that church is. As religious ideas, although referring to one and the same reality, can differ in form in different churches, so too with piety (or the pious mind); devotion, also, can mean one thing in this church and another in that.

#270

In itself, piety is an internal matter within individuals and within a church as a whole. But like all inner realities, it seeks expression and outward form in individuals and in the whole. Devotion, as piety's means of furtherance, is partly internal and partly external. Within the pious individual the expression of his piety and his devotion are never defined; both are completely free and conditioned by his individual circumstances. But within a church and for a church the expression of its piety and its whole devotional life are definable. Both are defined by the same spirit of piety which reigns in all the members of that church and by their common responsiveness to the same devotional means. Only to the extent that this common spirit and this common responsiveness are present in a community of pious persons can its piety find one and the same expression and one and the same devotional life. When the outward expression of inward piety and external devotion which is internally effective are united we call it worship. Thus, in conformity with its end, every church has formal worship and, as it develops, it must create such forms of worship for itself.

> * The forms of worship constitute *liturgy* and *ritual*. So, for the sake of its worship, the second thing which a church must possess is its liturgy.

#271

A church lives through its piety; it nourishes its spiritual life through its worship. But through neither of these, nor through its faith, does it yet possess its being, i.e., it does not possess through them any enduring existence in time and space. If it wants to attain this, it can do so only through a *polity* by which, as a religious society, it can insure that its members will remain united and work in unison for its ends, just as any other society established for other ends must insure its existence. This polity defines first of all how far one person in the church may assert his individual opinion in matters of religion over against the whole community and how far he must sacrifice it to the ends of the whole community which are also his ends, i.e., it defines his rights within the church. —But since a church as a religious society stands over against other communities of a similar kind and preeminently the state which embraces them all, the polity established for a church's preservation must also define its rights within the state. Thus the third thing which any church must have is its polity.

#272

What has been said thus far applies to all churches in general and for general reasons, and so to the Christian church as well. As a requirement for its existence, it must possess a common religious tradition embodied in a creed, as has already been discussed. As a requirement of its end, it must possess a common worship embodied in its liturgy. As a requirement for its existence in time and space, it must possess its polity embodied in organic forms. The discussion of these two latter requirements is found in the system of the Christian church. What is distinctive is only that people did not accidentally come to agreement on all three components of the Christian church. Doctrine, worship, and polity were not the creation of the first members who made up a Christian church but rather were given by one person—the Founder of the church—to them and to everyone so that, if they chose, they could be joined to the church which he created.

> * So, too, the scientific construction of the Christian church is by no means arbitrary; it can proceed only on the basis of the elements which have been *given*.

#273

As in Christian doctrine dogma is distinguished from opinion, so in Christian worship (in fact, in any worship) the essential is distinguished from the non-essential; the first is its fixed element, the second its mutable element (#256). What is essential in worship is precisely the pious awakening and conversion of the heart by the Holy through which transformed dispositions are effected within the person which lead him ever closer to God and to his true relationship to God. The conversion of the heart and the transformed dispositions which are produced by it, as well as the actual way they were produced, are purely inner realities which in themselves can never be available to the senses. Consequently, in contrast to what in worship is available to the senses, they are reckoned as *mysteries* or *sacraments*.

#274

What is non-essential is the expression and the sign of the sacrament. By this is meant either that through which the heart's inner awakening and conversion is sensibly expressed in a suitable manner, or that through which the heart is gently addressed from without, thanks to the analogous relationship between the inner world and the outer, or even the way in which the mystery works. In this last meaning of the term, the sign is actually a *symbolic act* which, for the sake of its significance, must be continuously present, like the sacrament. Anything in worship that is non-essential is called a *rite* and, in as much as it is not a symbolic act, a *ceremony*. —As the first part of the system of the Christian church, the theory of Christian worship has thus to distinguish and explain sacraments and rites.

> * Were it not customary to understand by *liturgy* the externals of worship and by *liturgics* the theory of those externals, these terms could be used for worship in general.

#275

As Christianity's doctrine and its church are things given or positive, so, too, is its worship. Nor is this worship merely historically given; its essence is also defined by the ideas of Christian doctrine. The root idea of that doctrine is the Kingdom of God, and the key ideas of the doctrine mark the great moments of the Kingdom through which it expands and achieves its fulfillment (#263* [apparently a mistake for #264*]). The church is the temporal and sensible manifestation of the Kingdom in which the key ideas of Christianity attain reality (#268). The religious life of the church consists in what worship clearly demonstrates and causes (#269), namely that what is proclaimed in doctrine as an idea here becomes reality. What in doctrine is proclaimed as an objective fact with universal significance within an intelligible world is in worship made present again to every individual in the church and becomes a subjective fact within the heart. The individual experiences the destiny of the whole world. There are as many key ideas in Christian doctrine as there are sacraments of Christian worship or functions in the spiritual life. —This is the significance of Christian worship scientifically considered and with reference to doctrine, which is the foundation of the whole system. This is the scientific construction of its theory.

#276

From this comes the more precise scientific concept of a sacrament as well as the connection of worship to ethics (#195), which can never be separated from worship. The functions of the spiritual life, in which the key ideas of Christianity are realized in the individual and in which the eternal law of the supersensual world which has been proclaimed under the image of the Kingdom of God is made present to the individual—these functions begin with an act which is as such a transcendental fact and can no more be brought to full clarity in human consciousness than the act with which physical life begins or those other acts from which spring the metamorphoses of physical life can be conscious of themselves. They are first perceived in their effects. These acts are thus true mysteries and can only be made apprehensible to human senses by a simultaneous phenomenon which informs and guarantees that the transcendental act has actually occurred at the same time. As a sign, and certainly as a powerful and meaningful sign, this phenomenon is itself an action—a symbolic action. So the transcendental act is bound to the symbolic action or sacrament; the first is the essence and the mystery, the second its expression.

#277

Every act—and thus, this transcendental act—induces as its immediate consequence in the human heart a *disposition*, and this, if it is not negated by an opposite disposition but becomes habitual and constant, again produces as its effect a *pattern of action* which makes itself known in perceptible actions of external life and forms an *ethic*. Thus worship, whose essence is the sacrament, comes together with ethics as the outward form of inner religious life. Science has to demonstrate theoretically this connection which in the praxis of worship is so readily apparent, namely that, according to its nature and definition, worship exerts such an influence on Christian ethics that it becomes its root and sustaining source. Likewise, faith, by which alone a sacrament can be understood, is confirmed by becoming actually perceptible through its actualization in ethics.

> *   Here it can be seen how the system of doctrine coincides with that of the Christian life. What appears in speculative doctrine as a pure idea is seen in Christian worship as a transcendental act; what was there a

practical maxim appears as ethics here. And just as there one and the same idea could be viewed under its speculative and its practical aspects, so here one and the same act is viewed under its transcendental and empirical aspects. But it seems necessary to discuss the scientific construction of the theory of the Christian life at somewhat greater length because it is seldom done.

#278

If the purpose of Christian worship is to stimulate and support in the human being a spiritual life in accord with the ideas of Christianity, then the theory of that worship must construct and explain its ritual as a means to that end. For whatever the externals and non-essentials in worship may be (#274), they can only be regarded as means, since worship has meaning and value only by referring us to what is internal and essential. In the most general terms, the principle of this construction is the dualism of the human being by which he is at once both a spiritual and a sensual being, which is the basis for an immediate relation between the external and the internal, the spiritual and the sensual. In terms of religion or piety, this general principle is given greater precision in that the Holy, to the degree that it can be seen in external sensuous phenomena, can only appear in the form of beauty. Thus, in its objective reference, ritual comes entirely under the heading of art.

#279

So, in this respect there is a general and complete construction of ritual. But as to the effect of ritual on any given heart, that is always an individual matter dependent on particular persons and occasions. Consequently, a theory of ritual may indeed be worked out for certain occasions and persons, but it can never be made universal. Although this holds true for general principles, with their aid theories pertaining to individual situations are constructed; therefore, only these come truly and necessarily under the theory of ritual.

#280

To apply these principles in evaluating an existing rite and its features at a specific point in time, the following basic rules are important. Since effectiveness of liturgical forms—as channels of devotion—depends on their power of significance (the reference of the external to the internal) and their aesthetic value, and since the concepts which mediate that significance and the aesthetic sense which mediates that value necessarily alter with the course of time, so too must liturgical forms alter. Thus, in any age only those rites will be effective and be retained which correspond to the level of development of religious ideas and to aesthetic tastes in religion and to religious needs generally. These religious needs are not determined by particular individuals, however, but by the majority of the members of the religious community; for worship exists for the community first of all, not for the individual.

#281

Thus the theory of ritual is also a critique which exhibits in established forms those elements which have held good until now but no longer meet religious needs and evaluates the adequacy of their proposed substitutes. Even more importantly, as a critique it must correct the confusion of mistaking the non-essential for the essential, the superficial appearance of life for real life, and the means of devotion for genuine devotion itself. For in these ways appearance replaces truth, whether it does so in the form of devotionalism or fanaticism or superstition. For all these follow upon one error, that of mistaking the non-essential in the spiritual life for the essential, and all find their correction in the theory of religious life. —Religious hypocrisy does not come from error but from perversity of will and so must look to moral theology for its correction.

> *   There should properly have been discussion of intellectual errors in reference to true religion in the first part of this theory which deals with the essence of Christian religious life. But since this is the first place we have been able to address the critical part of the said theory, we have placed together all the errors which this critique must correct.

#282

In other respects, what has been said about the elements of Christian doctrine in #256 holds true of the elements of Christian life. The essential is the fixed element of the Christian life, the non-essential the mutable. The only difference which must be added is that non-essentials, since they are purely external, can never become essentials or internal issues, whereas by contrast ideas which have attained their finished form and those which still stand in need of development are fully alike in their nature and therefore ideas of the second kind can at some future point be included among those of the first. This difference apart, what has been said about the study of Christian doctrine in #258 to #262 can, for the reasons given, be applied to the study of the theory of the Christian life.

#283

Specific mention must be made here of the analogy which holds between the two studies on the point of their adequacy. As in dogmatics symbolics and scholasticism stand contrasted as imperfect forms of the science and in moral theology mysticism and casuistry, so until now the theory of worship has been divided into two branches; that which deals with the essence of worship—sacraments—has been included under the system of doctrine (in dogmatics or in moral theology), and the other which contains the theory of non-essentials—ritual—has been treated under so-called liturgics. The distinction between essential and non-essential elements seems to justify this division. —But science which maintains the ideal of a complete theory of Christian worship, the nature of liturgics which can only treat all non-essential elements within it by reference to essential elements, and even accidental circumstances, all encourage the reintegration of what has been divided, i.e., a complete scientific study of everything which pertains to Christian worship, even though—as with the study of doctrine (#261)—such a study must necessarily be revised with time. Cf. #280.

#284

As a real and objective community, a church can only exist through a polity (#271); thus it must either possess a polity or be given one. —Now, it is true that in recent times the following claim has been made: "Justice is whatever accords with the contingencies of the external existence of the human being *qua* human being (whether the human being is taken by himself, in isolation and under no restraints or as under restraints in a society, or whether these societies are themselves taken by themselves in isolation or in interaction with other societies). Now, since the church's end is not external existence but something loftier, there is no religious justice, no church law. —The church is a community rooted in faith and love and so in freedom; thus there is within it no rule or government. —No known form of polity applies to the church; therefore, it can have no polity."

> * It is remarkable how, side by side with these basic principles on a polity for the church, people can still speak of a creed, a liturgy, and doctrines of the church.

#285

By contrast, it seems to us that one who limits justice simply to *the authorization of the satisfaction of the needs of human existence by the acquisition of external things* has a very limited concept of justice. Through the acquisition of external things the human being maintains his earthly existence. But this existence is not the ultimate end of the human being, nor is it his proper end; it is within religion that humanity's ultimate end is found, the end to which the religious person subordinates earthly existence as a means. So, if the human being has an undeniable right to his existence and to the means to the same, then he must have a similar right to the ultimate end of his existence and to the means to this end. And as in the first case a right confers on him the further authorization to force someone who would hinder him in the exercise of his rights to desist, so he must have a similar right to use force in the second case. Should he find himself in a community in which the assembled members have surrendered their right to use force in the first case for the sake of greater security, he cannot retain his right to use force even in the second case without contradicting that community and himself. He must also surrender the right to use force to that community on the obvious condition that the community will employ it for his protection. But he has ceded to the community—the state—only this right to use force, not his rights in general; otherwise, he would have left himself without any rights in a community possessing all rights. This is the individual's *religious* rights. If one substitutes for individuals a union of many persons for religious purposes, then we are dealing with the church's rights.

> * Thus the church has rights and retains them even within the state, save that it has no right to employ force, since it is not a physical power.

#286

The church is grounded in faith, as we have noted (#268), and faith when it is active and living shows itself as love, which human reason first learned from the Gospel. The church thus lives in love (cf. #263*). Faith, like love, is free, i.e., neither can be coerced by physical force. But truth has a moral force: its acceptance, i.e., a force which leads to faith. The good has a moral force: practical acceptance, i.e., a force which leads to love. Thus, acceptance is the *obligation* corresponding to the truth, and love the *obligation* corresponding to the good. And so if authority and government mean only some kind of coercion by physical force, then for the two reasons noted, there is no authority and no governance in the church. But if there is also such a thing as authority through suasion of faith and love, then there is authority in the church. And there is most certainly within it a *common will* which on the basis of a *common faith* strives for a *common end* by *common means*. Now since the authentic concept of governance is that the common will of a community is determined and directed toward the attainment of its common end, there must certainly be governance in the church. Further, since the basis of the church is different from that of the state, its end is different, its means are different and its common will is different, determination and direction of the will of the state is not at all the same as determination and direction of the will of the church; in other words, the *state* has its own *unique* style of government and the church has its own equally *unique* style of government. The two are distinct and separate.

#287

The way in which the common will in a community is formed and determined and the way in which, once determined, it is directed (or effected and applied), are called the constitution of a community and its form of polity. And here we find the well-known forms of government: simple and mixed. No one can be said not to belong to the church, so long as it is always recognized, as it must be recognized, that anyone who enters the church does so not under coercion but from free conviction and, once in it, can leave it again if some development within it is opposed to his conviction. Whatever may be said—and especially now a great deal is said—about the applicability of the forms of the state and its administration to the church rests on confusing that personal conviction which alone is inviolable and inalienable with all the beliefs which are not in contradiction to it and which very definitely can be abandoned and delegated. There is one thing which cannot be abrogated by any social contract and which each individual reserves to himself when he enters such a contract—the dignity of the human person.

#288

These are the general principles concerning the church's polity. When the polity of a positive and historical church is under discussion, as is now the case with the Christian church, then these principles can only serve as critical guidelines, for the polity of such a church can only be known historically. Scientifically constructing such a polity does not in any way mean devising any polity one wishes for church but is rather studying the data in terms of the idea of the church and in terms of its ends and means so that they can be understood as necessary to it. —Now our concern must be to note the outstanding subjects which the theory of church polity includes.

#289

And here the first point to observe is that the Christian church's polity must be viewed from two angles: from the first, it can be regarded in isolation as a unique and closed religious society; from the second, it is seen in its relation to the state, since as an ethical community its physical base cannot be within itself but only within the state. The church's polity considered from the first angle can be called its *internal* polity, considered from the second, its *external* polity.

#290

Not only if the Christian church had adopted its *internal* polity on its own but even if it had devised it, i.e., if the first Christians had made up their religious feelings, set up their doctrines on their own authority, decided on religious ends to suit themselves and a form of church to match those ends, even in that case it would have to be acknowledged that the Christian church had adopted this structure autonomously and that it was thus autonomous as regards the state and independent of the state's administration (##285–287). How much more, then, must this be acknowledged of the Christian church when its first members agreed that the foundations of their ecclesial life—their religious system (#268)—and the basic lines of its polity were given by divine authority. And so the Christian church has been constituted independently of any other authority. —At least, this is the first principle of the Christian church's catholicism, from which the second follows naturally: that any alteration in that original church polity, thus any alteration in its autonomy, is a denial of the Christian church itself, and whoever makes such an alteration dissociates himself from it.

#291

Apart from this unique quality of the Christian church, it must contain within it the essential elements of any ecclesiastical institution, and the theory of the polity of the Christian church has to determine how it does so. The first of these elements is the *creed* yielded by its doctrine to the extent that it is fixed (#262). The theory of the polity of the Christian church has thus to determine how the creed came into being in its primitive form, how it developed in response to later needs and circumstances, how it was given greater precision and so changed, in what ways it came to be accepted as the common position of all, and how, besides its subjectively free interpretation, its ecclesially authorized interpretation was established.

#292

The second element of every ecclesiastical institution is its *worship* and its *liturgy*. These have a theory devoted to them in their own right. In the theory of the polity of the Christian church the same issues are discussed regarding these as are mentioned above regarding the creed: namely, through what measures the essence of Christian worship has been preserved within the church, and how its accidental form, the liturgy, has been able to be changed so that its form as it has existed at any particular time has been accepted as the consensus of all while not infringing on peoples' subjectively free response of the heart.

#293

The third element is the political form of church government itself or the *hierarchy*. On this subject, the theory of the Catholic church's polity has first to determine general questions and then special ones. —The general questions are these: how and why is there a common will in the church of Christ which is completely positive?; how and why is there any direction given to this common will?; and through what universal organic structures is this decided and directed? And since a community's common will, once determined, is called its law, and the law is administered partially by the executive office and partially by the judicial, the theory of the Christian church has to demonstrate that three offices exist within the church and that there is an organic relation among them.

> * The church is not a physical power and so has no means of physical coercion (#285). But if it had no means whatever of supporting the order which exists within it, it would always be on the verge of dissolution. The church cannot call upon the state's power of physical coercion and its means of coercion because this would be both wrong and useless—wrong, because there is no room for coercion in matters of religion and so the state ought to apply none; useless, because physical coercion does not touch the spirit. Thus the church can employ no means for maintaining its order save moral ones, i.e., those which rely upon faith and the soul's requirements. When it withholds from one who destroys its order a part of its means for spiritual life, it works on him through the demands of his interior life and through the pain of conscience and so employs moral coercion on him. Such a withholding is as justifiable as the withholding of earthly goods by which the state applies coercion in its sphere. But the church does not aim merely at cessation of the action disruptive of its order and so the peace of the whole community as the state does in its punitive acts; through the nature of its means of coercion it aims at the interior betterment of the one punished. The goal of ecclesiastical punishment and coercion is thus pedagogical in nature—*training* or *discipline*. And so the greatest and final punishment which the church employs is excommunication.

#294

These general issues, i.e., the existence of these responsibilities and the way Christ has organized them within his church, constitute the essence of church government. As a positive church it must have such an essence, otherwise there would be no way of designating it at all, for everything is designated according to its essence. And this essence must continue in the church if it is to exist, for everything ceases to be as it departs from its essence. It is, therefore, necessary for this science to give a clear account of this essence and to maintain it in the church's life.

#295

A distinction must be drawn between the essence of an ecclesial polity and those elements which have been accommodated to its essence from without in the ongoing development of the church's life and which are to be regarded as products of changed times and circumstances. Such non-essentials must be incorporated into the church from time to time to supplement its polity and render it workable in a particular age, and so the Christian church, being positive, has had to do this. It has had to do so because it has had to accommodate itself to this or that period, and what has been suitable at one time, just as what had been suitable at earlier times, could not be permanent. It has had to do so because, founded as the universal church for all ages and nations, it has had to maintain its ability to incorporate all within itself and to exert its influence on all.

#296

Distinguishing these non-essential, merely temporary elements in the Christian church's polity necessarily belongs to the scientific theory of that polity. Obviously not everything which was ever present and important in the Christian church's polity is material to the theory. A large part is the subject matter of history; the theory has to deal only with what is now the case. But as a scientific theory it must not study an issue simply because it is currently the case; it must show how this present element agrees with the essence of church government on the one hand and with the temporal and local needs of the church on the other. And so it is also its task to make clear when some existing situation is no longer suitable either to the essence of church government or to the church's needs and so must be changed.

#297

These non-essentials are also particular ways of arranging the church's polity (#293), which can refer not only to different times in the church but also to different places at the same time (national churches, etc). These particular arrangements can, of course, be found in all branches of the church's organization but are especially strongly marked in its form of government, i.e., the way and style in which church offices are divided up following its essential and original polity and made subject to mutual checks and the ways in which various ecclesiastical offices interact toward the end to which the whole church is oriented.

> * The distinctions propounded from #291 on are also the basis for the differentiation of a universal, general, and special church law. These have been largely confused in studies until now—polity and legal decisions, the essential and the accidental, current situations and past ones, the general and the particular, as well as a mass of historical data which have become topics in church law and which do not belong there at all. It is much to be desired that now, when in the course of time the church has been restored to its true self and has to re-establish its general polity, thoughtful and well-intentioned people winnow through this long-standing chaos and set forth a well-grounded system of Catholic church polity and its laws from which those who are collaborating on this renewal can seek guiding principles when they want.

#298

The external polity of the church includes the establishment of its relations vis-à-vis the state. These relations arise from the different roles which the church and the state play. Where these are acknowledged and to the extent they are acknowledged, there and to that degree one can talk about mutual relations. But when the church and the state are thought of as one and the same or as one within the other, then the concept of relationship is discarded. Thus the basis of all inquiries of this type is the presupposition that the church and the state are not one and the same and not one within the other, but two separate realities side by side.

> * The concept of the two being side by side also excludes that of being one under the other (coordination cannot be subordination). For to the degree that one thing is subordinated to another, it is only a tool or organ of that other, and thus something which belongs to it and is a part of it.

#299

The opposition of church and state cannot be resolved in a purely rationalistic way or on an ideal basis alone. For the rationalized state nowhere exists just as the rationalized church nowhere exists, and so universal solutions apply everywhere and nowhere. There exist only particular empirical churches and particular empirical states, which carry within themselves their ideas, of course, but express them always in their own peculiar ways. These peculiarities are simply historical givens and are knowable only as such, and from them more than from general ideas are the opposition and therefore the relations of states and churches to one another to be resolved. Consequently, the relation of one and the same church is not the same to all states and vice-versa.

#300

Still there are general elements present in all churches and states, and these general elements yield the forms under which are brought the particular relations between churches and states and in which they may be studied. Only these general forms can be noted in an encyclopedic study in which the actual theory of the polity of the Christian church has to set forth the relations of that church to currently existing states.

#301

The typical relation in which the Christian church stands to all states—societies—is certainly not a hostile one. It can only be understood on the basis of its key religious insight: *the Kingdom of God—among human beings*. The highest end at which any society organized into a state can aim—and each in its own way—is the establishment of the authority of earthly law within a nation. The church is concerned with and seeks to realize the highest end which is given to *human beings*, and this for all people without distinction and in the same way. The church is everywhere the same. The state is concerned with and seeks to realize the highest end which is given to *citizens* and everywhere in different ways; states and peoples are always different from one another. The Christian church and the state are thus related as a universal human reality and a national one, as a heavenly reality and an earthly one. Both ideas are independent but neither eliminates the other; rather, both must stand side by side, though one is unattainable by the other.

#302

This is the Christian church in its idea. If it could remain purely within the ideal realm, purely within the domain of thought, it would remain unattainable in every respect by the state, and there could be no problem between it and the state. But the church, i.e., its members, must also act, and every (external) act falls within the sphere of the state; consequently, so does the church. Thus in the eyes of the state it is a public association (or corporation) with a special purpose and in general stands in the same legal relation to the state as other such associations. Particular institutions hold legal standing in the state through being recognized as ecclesiastical corporations. These legal relations are mutual, however, and so a theory of external church polity has to deal with them.

#303

What the church can demand from the state in this regard is, first of all, total independence in its internal polity, so that the only choice the state has is to exclude the church if the state does not like it or grant the church as it exists full civil rights. This is the negative right of the church vis-à-vis the state. Any middle course is tyranny, an encroachment on rights which do not belong to the state. It is self-evident that still less can the state persecute a church and that no church can claim more civil rights than another.

#304

When the church is recognized as a religious corporation by the state, then it has as an immediate result freedom for any action required by its internal polity and enjoys the protection of the state against any intrusion in this regard. This is the positive right of the church vis-à-vis the state. It remains for the theory of the external polity of the church to demonstrate that this freedom and protection for whatever pertains to the church's internal polity—such as the creed, liturgy, and hierarchy—also extends to whatever external and accidental goods and institutions the church possesses.

#305

But if the state has found the internal polity of the Christian church—or any aspect of it—both in its idea and its end fully compatible with its own proper end and has thus extended to it full civil rights, the possibility still remains that members of the church might threaten the rights and well-being of the state, even though this would be totally against the mind of the church itself. And the church can offer no guarantee for the behavior of its members. So the state has the right to repel any encroachment on its own independence and well-being made under the pretense of being an act of the church and to protect itself from harm. This is the negative right of the state vis-à-vis the church.

#306

From this negative right and especially from the fact that the church may certainly deplore attacks on the state's welfare by individual members but cannot prevent them is derived the right of the state to protect itself against the church and to exercise oversight not only on the actions of individuals which could seriously damage the state but also on changes which the church may find advantageous to introduce into its polity as the state has recognized it until then. This is the positive right of the state vis-à-vis the church; it is, as can be seen, a police right.

> * Every right of the state finally comes down to a matter of policing, which it can use against the church, or rather against individuals within the church, either as a right of punishment or as a right of self-protection. It is an essential concern of a theory of church polity to define the limits of the state's exercise of police law over the church; but it is not easy to do so, because this police function, like most others of the same sort, is necessary on the one hand but dangerous and odious on the other. We might summarize this branch of the theory of church polity in this way: in whatever concerns the mutual rights and obligations of the church and the state with regard to (temporal) goods which the church may possess or acquire, since these goods are the church's *property* but not an *essential element* of the church, the church stands in relation to the state in the same way as any other corporation. Thus this whole question belongs to the study of law.

#307

Whatever is said about a theory of church-state relations always remains on the level of general relations which are greatly modified in any given state by its political structure and national character (#299). Within the theory, these particular considerations appear as accidentals. These relations also change when the polity of the state or the church changes, and neither of these can remain unchanged forever.

As often as such changes occur, strains must appear in the peaceful relations of the church and state, and the deeper those changes go, the more painful will those strains be. They are to be resolved only through new settlements between state and church; the concept of *concordats*, therefore, is a necessary part of the theory of church polity. And it does not require much thought to see that any time a concordat is *negotiated* between the state and the church, it applies to the church only as it exists *within that state*. For if the church exists within other states as well and has its center outside the state in question—as does the Catholic church—then this church is of concern to the state only to the extent that it exists within it. How the local church relates to the universal church of which it is a part and to its center is a purely ecclesiastical matter about which the state can neither know nor do anything.

B.3. Study of Scientific Theology

#308

The general character of scientific theology is set out in #63ff. —The method of its treatment and its study as a whole and in particular divisions can only be scientific. What pertains to this method in general is determined in philosophy because it is the formal theory of science. Here we can indicate only how general scientific method has to be employed on the given content of Christian theology in the course of its study.

#309

The application of the scientific method to a given subject matter presumes the scientific mind-set. This is, therefore, the first point to be noted in the study of scientific theology. But it cannot be learned or taught; it can only be gained, presuming a natural aptitude and a natural cast of mind, through thinking and acting on one's own. It is clear from what has already been said that an authentically scientific understanding of the contents of Christian theology is not for everyone and that scientific theology, although necessary in the full system of theology, is not a requirement for every theologian. The individual will find the touchstone for his talents in this regard to be whether he finds himself driven to understand any given claim of historical theology as necessary by the standards of his reason. This understanding systematically pursued is the scientific study of theology in its proper and most rigorous sense.

#310

Distinct from this, although in a sense still scientific, is that study of the doctrines of the Christian religion in which, once understood from a purely historical perspective, these doctrines are organized and combined by reflection and logical skill in such a way that the natural interconnection of all the ideas becomes obvious and understandable. Such a study and organization of ideas are generally called systematic, and so theology in this form is known as systematic theology, which until now has been the name of this branch of theological study. But systematic theology or systematics is simply the formal, architectonic aspect of the science, which is the same for every science, whatever its content is. —Precisely for this reason the demand can be placed on anyone who pretends to scientific education that he possess his theological knowledge, even if it is actually only historical knowledge, in a systematic form or that he render it in that form.

#311

Of course, he will lay the foundation for this by attending a course of lectures on systematic theology or familiarizing himself with one of the best textbooks on the subject. This can only be done with an eye to making an initial attempt at systematically organizing the doctrines of the Christian religion, and from this point of view, it does not much matter what the initial model is which is used for the attempt; but some model must be used. Anyone who perseveringly engages in reflection on Christian systematics (and that will be someone impelled by inclination and vocation) will soon discover that systematics can be constructed in various ways and will design his own style of construction.

#312

Internal or real construction is important, of course, but also difficult. Here everything depends on disengaging Christianity *as given* from its accidental form in which it looks to ordinary historical view like every other given reality and knowing how to elevate all of it to the perspective in which it can be understood as a necessary phenomenon. But if this perspective is to be not merely a so-called historical-pragmatic one but a truly scientific perspective, then the construction of Christianity cannot be based on phenomena preceding or coexisting with it, as some have thought, or on ordinary principles of historical construction, in fact not on any historical approach whatever; it must be based on ideas alone. —And since we are dealing with religious knowledge or the science of religion, these must be religious ideas which see all things in terms of their relation to God. —Finally, since Christianity concentrates all religious ideas into one unique idea and has cast this idea in a particular form, all the individual doctrines of Christianity when raised to the level of ideas must be explained in terms of that one idea. In this way the science of religion will be authentically Christian and differentiated from several other possible and similar scientific constructions. —This is all that can be said at this point about the nature and procedure of the method of internal construction of the science with which we are dealing.

#313

So its crucial point is the construction of the root idea or real principle of Christian theology and of the key doctrines immediately derived from it. This construction and derivation are done in the foundational studies of the science. I maintain that these foundational studies are the most important for the scientific understanding of Christianity. For other concerns in theological studies, other branches or other issues within these same branches may be more important. But once one is equipped to deal with Christian theology scientifically, then he can decide whether the construction and derivation we have described matter to the degree stated in the foregoing paragraph.

#314

In apologetics and polemics properly so-called, purely scientific construction is already in service of the will and of a practical orientation. No longer is it simply and solely knowledge, rather it is the importance of what is known and of the truth which drives the theologian to proclaim in apologetics his beliefs about Christianity and the value of his church and to maintain in polemics what he has proclaimed against existing opposed views. Apologetic and polemical theology rely upon a scientific foundation in the most rigorous sense, and their success depends on its worth. This is further inducement to those whose keen interest or special role in the church may make them into apologists or polemicists to ground their views on the essence of Christianity and the church scientifically.

#315

Since in apologetics and, for the most part, in polemics everything revolves about the contradictions between what is essential and the positive data and since the contradictions within the positive data themselves in the domains of religion and the church can be truly understood and resolved only in terms of the relationship between the positive data and what is essential, the beginning student in the science must regard a basic understanding of those contradictions, or better, of the appearance of contradictions, as the first requirement for any true and solid progress in these branches of his study. He will only be able to achieve this, however, through the construction in which he learns to see what is given accidentally as a necessary reality. For it is all one and the same contradiction, the contradiction between the accidental and the necessary and that between positive data and what is essential, because what is positive about the positive data in religion can only refer to their origin and their givenness and their necessity to the essence of the human being and his natural orientation to God.

#316

If the scientific study of theology in all the foundational branches must confine itself more to the general, and thus to ideas and basic principles, in *specialized* science it is directed to the particular, to the system worked out in the complete range of its conceptual formulae. Here ideas which are necessary and essential retreat into the background, and in turn, conceptual formulae which are accidental and positive come to the fore. Specialized science is necessarily historical because all particular conceptual formulae, which are various expressions of ideas, can only arise and assume their form at some particular point in time and without reference to that point in time are unintelligible. Indeed, specialized science would become completely empirical were the conceptual formula not understood as an expression of an idea or at least not seen in terms of its systematic deduction from, and its connection with, other conceptual formulae. Since we cannot expect every theologian to be capable of that first way of dealing with conceptual formulae (##309, 313), only the second way of dealing with them is required of every theologian (#310).

#317

From the brief discussion which has been given of specialized science, it can readily be seen that the study of specialized science must commence with the study of *doctrine*—of speculative doctrine, in fact—or of *dogmatics*. But since dogmatics stands in a necessary relation to the church, it is self-evidently clear and natural that each theologian must first become familiar with the doctrine of *his* church. He can only become familiar with it, however, if he has done so *completely*, i.e., the study of doctrine ought not be only the study of the creed (#262); it must be a genuine study of dogmatics.

#318

In regard to doctrine, however, the theologian must not be motivated by knowledge alone; he must be motivated by his commitment to what is known. First, he must be motivated by what he studies. For it is truth, all-important—that is to say, religious—truth; this is what it claims to be, and it demands that one seek to be committed to it. Then he must be motivated by his religious character. For this should indeed be the end result of religion, that it builds character; but character is the fruit of commitment. Any person necessarily lacks character to the degree that he is without personal commitment. Lastly, he must work for the sake of the church. A person belongs to a church because he shares his religious commitment in common with it (#268). One can work within and for a church only to the extent that he does so *forcefully*, for the force of an act comes from faith, *morally*, for any act which is not rooted in personal commitment is sin, and *lawfully*, for only under this condition does the church assign him a place to work within its domain.

> * Wherever inquiry for its own sake is taken to be the highest task of theological study, the spirit of the science has fallen into decay; wherever doubt is extolled as the highest rule for this study, religious life has fallen into decay; wherever doubt and lack of ecclesial faith are found united to a teaching office in the church, ecclesial life has fallen into decay along with religious life.

#319

As for the breadth of knowledge of Christian doctrine which one must possess, it is clear that it is not asking too much to expect the theologian to have full knowledge of the fixed element of doctrine (#256), of the mutable element from which further development of the fixed element may be anticipated (#259), and of the divergent doctrines of other confessions which either still exist as an alternative or, if they no longer actually exist, have had such an influence on the doctrines of his own church that they can now be fully understood only with reference to those alternative positions. —Opinions which have disappeared without leaving a trace within the science do not occupy the same level as what has been mentioned and do not enjoy the same importance in the study of the science (#259*); they may, however, be pertinent to its study for anyone who wishes to have as perfect a knowledge of the history of the science as possible.

* What is said here applies with equal force to both aspects of doctrine, the practical as well as the speculative.

#320

As the theory of the church depends on the system of doctrine, it follows immediately upon the study of doctrine. Without having grasped the doctrine of Christianity scientifically one can understand nothing of worship and church polity scientifically. Since the ideas of Christianity are realized in the church, the first task of the scientific study of its theory is to form a clear picture of how religious ideas enter into life: first creating internally and subjectively certain dispositions within the individual, then making themselves known externally and objectively and uniting like-minded individuals who externalize their feelings in similar ways into a visible religious society—a church. Once one has understood this in general—and this can be done only through the principles of religious ethics—one will easily apply this to uniquely Christian ideas and so will be able to build a theory of Christian worship and of the church.

#321

Anything limited to a particular age and thus mutable in the externals of worship and church polity is for that reason not a subject for scientific understanding. It can only become a subject for this understanding when it is seen as the expression of an idea which is externalized in a manner appropriate to a particular age and as the development of one and the same spirit which ever re-forms itself. It is in this way that philosophical history has to evaluate and construct now vanished forms of worship and church polity and that science has to do the same with existing and still developing forms.

> * Through this strictly scientific construction, the student will be able to maintain the middle path between two parties which now stand resolutely in mutual opposition, between the *immobilists* (*les immobiles*) who always cling to whatever is antiquated and discarded by the Spirit and the *eccentrics* who manufacture for themselves innovations quite independently of the Spirit and want to exchange whatever is most ancient for whatever is most recent.

#322

As for the breadth of knowledge which one must possess in this branch of scientific theology, there are various opinions. —Beyond dispute, each must know whatever has been described as essentials in Christian worship and in the church (##273, 294) and know them in an authentically scientific manner whenever possible and at least in a historical manner whenever nothing else is possible (##320, 309). —As far as what were described as non-essentials (##274, 295), since questions both of time and geography come into play here (#297), each person must naturally have as full an understanding as possible of whatever the case is or is in process of becoming in worship and polity in that area of the church to which he directly belongs. This demands not only immediate application of science to the given situations, but also consideration of the theologian's practical obligations and his professional work within the church, which he can perform only in some definite locale. —This consideration calls for a distinction between the theories of worship and of polity. Anyone who has been called or expects to be called to a position of leadership within the church must know both theories fully. For church leadership consists primarily in maintaining worship and polity and constantly administering them in light of their ultimate purposes. If one's responsibility is almost exclusively concerned with worship, he must, of course, be thoroughly knowledgeable about its theory; the theory of polity is less necessary to him.

#323

In general, the remarks already made about the historical study of theology (#214) hold true for its scientific study. What can be gained during one's course of theological studies is only a general notion of the scientific study of theology, an ideal image of Christianity in its entirety, the general principles and method of its construction, and some exercise in their use. And while attaining this must be the student's goal, the teacher's task is to make the attainment of the goal possible for his hearers. The theologian may succeed in fully mastering his science only after long study, and perhaps never. So, too, in the course of continued study, he may find occasion and cause to abandon the system of the school in which he at first began.

III. Practical Theology

#324

The end of any church is religious life or piety or union of human beings with God (#269). This end appears in the Christian church in its characteristic idea of the Kingdom of God which is to be realized in and through it (#208). It fulfills this end through everything which is constitutive of it: through its creed in which it gives theoretical development to this idea; through its worship in which it creates and forms true citizens of that Kingdom; through its polity which is designed for the administration of the sources of its interior life. Thus far this polity has been examined on the theoretical level (##284–307). If it is to be effective, it must be translated into life and operate through *church officers* who undertake its work and act in its spirit. The theologian who wants to understand Christianity historically and scientifically in all its ramifications is instructed in how to administer the polity and act in its spirit in practical theology (##73, 74).

> * There is nothing objectionable in the notion of church officers. Anyone who sets himself some obviously necessary service as the purpose of his action finds that this purpose imposes an obligation upon him, and the fulfillment of that obligation is his office. This is all the more true if a society adds a positive obligation to this natural one.

#325

In any church, as in any society which has a political structure, there is a difference between *government* and *administration*. The first executes the polity within the community as a whole, the second applies it in particular instances. This difference is based on the nature of an organic unity in which the part exists within the whole and the whole exists above the part. From this view, church government is distinguished from church administration, and likewise the church officers whom we have mentioned are divided into *those exercising supervision of the church* and *those ministering within the church*, as they are traditionally described.

> * So they are called from their outward position and their kind of work in the church. In terms of their concerns and the inner spirit of their work, they are all called *clergy* [lit. *Geistliche*, "spirituals"] because by virtue of their charge they care for people's spiritual needs and, in order to do so, are supposed to be more advanced than others in religious life. These reasons for differentiating the spiritual leaders [clergy] from the laity should be obvious to everyone.

#326

The church confers the office, God confers the spirit of the office and its proper exercise, and what we have called practical theology adds helpful instruction. For it is certainly clear that such instruction is needed. The general reasons have already been noted in #73. But beyond them, the application of theoretical knowledge which is provided by the science as we have discussed up until now requires, in the actual execution of office, further special education. Even the gift of the Spirit, assuming that it is also present, can only operate in certain forms and through certain means, which a person discovers more easily when they are pointed out to him and which, since they are not left to his discretion, must be so pointed out. Further explanation of this last reason will be given below.

#327

The education which practical theology provides the clergy in the discharge of their offices falls into two lines of instruction following two aspects of the clerical office. There is (i.e., it can be imagined and ought to be the case that there would be) an introduction to the fruitful *discharge of the government of the Christian church* and an introduction to the fruitful *discharge of the service of the Christian church*.

> * What has been offered until now in so-called pastoral theology was actually only an instruction for the ordinary pastor or church minister. Protestant theologians needed no more, since there is no church

governance in their communities or what has gone under this title is so very limited. But that Catholic theology still lacks an introduction to the performance of church governance—an essential discipline according to its system—may stem either from theologians, who as a rule are in rank clergy of the lower order, not trusting themselves, due to fear, of instructing their superiors in how to carry out their offices, or from these superiors not asking for such instruction because of over-reliance on their, and perhaps God's, strength.

#328

What is common to both ecclesial governance and ecclesial ministry is that both are forms of work within the church for the advancement of its ends through the appropriate means. —In terms of what is common to them, both depend on the same conditions and the introductions to both on the same fundamental principles. The conditions for effective work within the church are its *spirit*, i.e., a purified sensitivity and vital attachment to the realization of the Kingdom of God among human beings, and *knowledge* of Christianity and the church. Without its spirit, any work within the church is powerless and haphazard; without knowledge, it is senseless and blind. How this spirit is obtained has already been noted in #326; science provides the knowledge. A practical introduction presumes both.

* Now, when the discussion concerns the introduction to the performance of the clerical office, it will not be out of order to underscore from this point of view the need for a scientific education. Without scientific knowledge, the doctrine, worship, and polity of the church cannot be maintained in the community at large, nor can this doctrine, worship, or church discipline be made fruitful in individuals. Without knowledge of the historical course of Christianity, the church's present situation cannot be understood from within, and without such an understanding neither on major nor on minor issues can the church be assisted opportunely toward the realization of its end. Thus education in the science is equally essential for one to exercise skillful supervision of the church and for the church's minister.

#329

The basic principles are also the same in both introductions. For although they are thoroughly practical and simply supply rules, the rules must still be drawn from fundamental principles. The principles of any act are determined by the nature of the act. Now, every act of church governance and of church ministry is by its very nature *a cure of souls*. All the clergy's activity is directed toward the soul exclusively; their highest concern is to further the good of souls, and the means to this end are purely spiritual. Thus, from every point of view, the basic principles from which practical theology derives its rules are principles of the cure of souls.

#330

But the rules which are derived from these common basic principles are different for church government and for the church's ministry. For the first deals with the whole church and the second with individuals within the church. And if the same means happen to be employed both in governing the church and in its ministry, still the way they are employed differs in the two cases. For church governance is concerned with preserving all the means through which the church attains its final ends and so with preserving the church itself; this is its purpose. But the ministry of the church makes these means available to individuals and so ultimately to the whole church, makes them as effective as possible, and so realizes very directly the church's ends; this is its purpose.

#331

From this the task of the two kinds of instruction into which practical theology is divided may now be more precisely defined. An introduction to church government offers guidelines drawn from the basic principles of the cure of souls dealing with the positive institutions of the church in order both to maintain the means to the church's ends and to form and refine them according to the church's circumstances in any given age—without detriment to their essential nature—so that they remain always as appropriate to those ends as possible. In the same way, an introduction to ministry in the church presents guidelines for applying the means present in the church to individuals in such a way that they may have the greatest possible effect on these souls and most perfectly fulfill their common purpose.

> * The notion given here of introductions to church government and to ministry in the church is now further developed. In this development

the guidelines themselves naturally cannot be given; only the key points about which the guidelines give direction and the basic principles from which the guidelines are drawn can be noted. But in terms of the guidelines themselves, it ought to be observed that they can be described with considerable generality for the governance of the church because the structure and the condition of the church as a whole are well enough known; the guidelines for ministry in the church must always have a very relative weight at best because they deal with individual cases so exclusively. Therefore, an introduction to church ministry must always remain incomplete, and much, indeed most, of what is important in this field must be left to the spirit and good sense of the pastor.

1. Introduction to Church Government

#332

Any introduction to church government must begin with the distinction between interior and exterior church polity (#289). For the administration of the church is based on its polity and its immediate purpose is to preserve whatever is intrinsic to that polity. An introduction to church government has therefore to provide guidelines for advancing the church's purposes through means found in the interior polity of the church, and second, for protecting those goals from any obstacle arising from the church's position over against the state. The first is the positive, the second the negative aspect of church government. If one is not overly nice in terminology, the first aspect can be called *ecclesiastical governance* and the second *ecclesiastical politics*.

#333

The chief topics of church governance and its central focus are the elements of church polity—creed, liturgy, the form of polity itself. They are the means through which the church strives to attain its end. The task of church governance is to preserve these means within the church and to render them effective and suitable to their purposes in every age. It accomplishes this task through wise laws which it provides for this task and through careful observance and application of these laws once they have been provided. —An introduction to ecclesiastical government thus appears in this regard to be an introduction into the legislative and executive work of the church in order to preserve and apply the creed, the liturgy, and the form of polity. —Only the most general points and principles which such training must take into account can be noted here.

#334

In safeguarding the creed the chief concern is that doctrine be kept pure, i.e., authentically Christian. This can be done only when doctrine rests on its historical basis—the means of its tradition—and this, in turn, is kept pure, that is, when anything which arises in opposition and contradiction to the spirit and doctrines of the creed is noticed and eliminated in such a way as to protect the creed. Thus this introduction has to determine, in accord with church polity, by what legislative and executive action the church can preserve the historical basis of its creed, spread it in an appropriate way, safeguard it against misuse, resolve disputes, and interpret the creed.

#335

But since the content of the creed—the ideas of Christianity—is understood in a progressive development and has to be understood in this way in order to build up the church (#256), ecclesiastical government has the responsibility to watch over the progressive development of doctrine and the form the creed at any given moment, to allow no obstacles to get in the way of the development of the church's doctrine, and also to take note of any development which is directed against the creed or which threatens and negates it, so as to forestall its destructive influence. Once again, this introduction teaches how this is to be accomplished through law and church discipline.

#336

Furtherance of religious life within the church depends especially on worship, the external forms of which are determined by the liturgy. Consequently, it is as important a task for church government to preserve the essence of worship as to preserve the creed. Legislative and executive responsibilities in this regard are easier than with respect to the creed because worship consists not in ideas but in actions, and by their nature these cannot have as mutable a form as the expression of ideas.

#337

On the other hand, since acts of worship are mysteries which are symbolized for those who are religiously sensitive in liturgical forms

(#276), the reality of worship depends in part on these forms. Thus training in church governance has to decide on the principles and rules which can guarantee reality to those forms over the course of changing times and circumstances. Basic principles in this regard are general and simple, but rules must always be determined according to time and circumstances.

> * The most general and simplest principles are as follows. It must be a maxim of all ecclesiastical government that no liturgical form and no formulary be allowed to exist beyond the limits of that time and those circumstances in which and from which they originated, for otherwise the liturgy loses both its significance and its reality. —But it must also be a maxim in church government to guard against continual instability and still more against violent and lawless reform of ritual. In the first case, no liturgy will ever take form, and in the second, its impact on the heart and behavior will be undermined. —So, the basic principle must be to introduce change into the liturgy more often but only very gradually. If ecclesiastical government fails to do this, it will necessarily fall into one of the two alternatives mentioned, and then we have a *real* problem! —Since the members of a church will always be at different levels in their education and religious needs, there can never be a liturgy which completely satisfies everyone within one and the same nation or still less within different nations. So here the principle must be the greatest possible balance between multiplicity and uniformity. —In the actual establishment of liturgical forms the prudence of the church's government, which tries to plan for the whole community, and the experience of the church's ministers, who attend to individuals, must interact. The former cannot leave it to the efforts of the latter alone, but neither can it omit listening to those most directly engaged in the liturgy.

#338

The third object of ecclesiastical legislation and government is the form of polity itself. As in the theory of polity what is essential and immutable is distinguished from what is accidental and mutable, so the task of ecclesiastical governance likewise has different responsibilities in regard to them. As far as essentials are concerned, attention must be aimed at preserving them; accidentals must be arranged so that the whole purpose of the polity—the church's well-being—is realized through them as securely as possible.

#339

Since in these aspects of its external form the church comes closest to secular government and so runs the danger that its governors might be infected with the disease of secular government—lust for power—to the church's immense detriment, an introduction to church government faces here its greatest and most difficult task: it must make the church's governors aware of the rocks on which their proper attitude and their blessed work could shatter and, at the same time, prescribe rules for avoiding those rocks.

#340

Here we can only mention those points to which this introduction must devote its greatest attention. Since the basis of all church polity is the distinction between the clergy and the people, but from *one* perspective this distinction always remains and must remain indefinite and so defined differently at different times, this introduction must provide guidelines by which one can know how sharp this distinction is or is not in fact and so whether the polity needs to underscore or cancel it. This is also true of the hierarchical grades as specific limits within which any ecclesiastical power may be exercised by those who are authorized to do so. Since only the essential form of the polity is immutable and within it the limits of offices, both for the well-being of the church itself and because of external circumstances, must sometimes be increased and sometimes diminished, sometimes expanded and sometimes contracted, this introduction has to decide when and how the form of hierarchical organization needs to be changed in accord with the church's various circumstances and stages and with what remains of abiding importance.

> * When the church's governors are infected with the worldly spirit of domination, they will want to focus attention on their rights vis-à-vis one another instead of attending exclusively to the ends of the church. And they will define these rights purely in terms of what existed and what was done in an earlier or later period rather than seeing the use of a right simply as a means to the church's ends and deciding according to this standard whether that right should now be exercised as it was of old.

#341

What has been said to this point about prudence in ecclesiastical government, especially with regard to the organizational and legislative functions, is to be understood in the same way of the administrative and executive functions. Since the church, in order to preserve itself, must and does have means to administer its existing organization (#293*), wisdom in church government consists in making the best use of church discipline. How this may be done this introduction must likewise teach.

> * The fundamental principles in this matter are: The church permits the pedagogical means of coercion included in its discipline to be used only to eliminate that which is diseased or alien (heterogeneous); it actually carries out this process of elimination only when what is diseased has proven incurable or when what is alien has proven incapable of assimilation. Before it cuts them off, it first seeks to heal the one and to incorporate the other. An introduction to church governance must, therefore, provide rules for employing the church's disciplinary means so that they function not merely as punishments, but as means of improvement.

#342

As mention has repeatedly been made, especially in #259, that there is within the church an analogy to what within the state is called public opinion, and as within the church this can only be the positions taken by officially recognized teachers and writers, so finally an introduction to church government must provide guidelines as to how the church can support this channel of opinion and what the correct attitude ought to be toward it.

> * Church history demonstrates that such a channel of opinion has always existed in the church. Explanation and inquiry by private scholars and authors always preceded the definitions of church doctrines, and most recommendations for improvements in the liturgy and in the church's discipline came not from the church's prelates but from zealous and wise private persons.

#343

The fundamental principle here is that church government neither can nor ought to suppress the activity and influence of individuals which are addressed to the church at large through the spoken or written word, because it would at the same time deprive itself of the devotion and insight inherent in the mass of its members. But neither can a church government acknowledge or admit an influence acting in this way which is not directed toward preserving and edifying the church. For in either of these opposed situations, the government would be working for its own and the church's dissolution. Thus there ought to be maxims for church governance such that free expression of religious zeal and insight can exist and yet the church can restrain through appropriate means the dangers which might possibly be incurred by this.

> * One should not confuse, however, free expression of *private* opinion in the church with that opinion which, without claiming this distinction for itself, has of its very nature a *public* character and is intended for *public* use.

#344

The chief considerations in ecclesiastical governance are the following. By the very nature of the case, the scientific element must predominate in the work of teachers and writers within the church. But the animating element in the church is not knowledge but practical religious life, and here church governance makes its appearance. In its wisdom it must find means to prevent religious life from being stifled for lack of scientific clarity but in such a way that the scientific element does not undermine the religious element and that science does not adopt a profane orientation but remains directed to what is of practical importance. —The scientific work of individuals is concerned with new developments and with criticism of whatever is old and currently the case. And in this way it cannot fail to happen that many useless, inappropriate, indeed, even destructive and wrong things will be uncovered which public opinion will recognize as being so. But the government of the church is concerned with conservation; its attention is fixed first and foremost on the fact and the importance of what is currently the case. Because of the conservative perspective from which it looks at everything, it must seek to avoid any break between the old and the new; in this perspective, the new must appear as simply another form of the old and even error as an imperfect grasp of the truth which it must accompany. For wise governance there must, therefore, be means to maintain continuity without impeding new developments and the improvements they bring with them and to avoid discarding truth with error and the church's foundations with its current forms. —Finally, as instruction and discussion always go on within definite limits beyond which they become unintelligible and so must prove unproductive, an introduction to church governance has to designate ways by which ecclesiastical government can prevent the discussion's overstepping those limits in some manner into areas where it would be inappropriate and destructive. In all the instances mentioned, the more clearly those charged with the supervision of the church and the channels of public opinion are aware of their roles and the limits of their work, the more harmoniously and peacefully will developments proceed in the church.

#345

As regards the church's position vis-à-vis the state (#332), the highest prudence in church governance consists in always keeping the church in its natural relation to the state (#301). This is the whole of its political program. Because this relation can be destroyed in two ways—either because the church through some action by large or small groups within it oversteps its proper sphere, or because the state within which the church is located does so—an introduction to church government has to provide guidelines for how the church can put a stop to either one or other.

#346

The church can more readily and directly prevent the first kind of trespass because it is its own act. All it requires on the part of those with oversight of the church is that they keep constantly in mind the proper mission of the church and that this is totally and essentially different from the mission of the state. Then the church could never seek to supplant the state, still less exalt itself above the state or subordinate the state to itself. If those charged with the church's supervision join to this constant awareness continual attention to their colleagues and to large and small communities within the church, then they will be wary of any trespass beyond the church's sphere and will ceaselessly keep them within their proper limits, as they certainly have authority to do.

* The vigilance of those who oversee the church must be exercised toward themselves and toward subordinate church officers especially

with regard to two temptations through which the church most easily falls—and as history shows, has fallen—into the danger of overstepping its bounds, namely, the temptation to power and the temptation to wealth. Through the first temptation the church can become so blind that it confuses its inner autonomy and independence with its external dependence on the state and, because it imagines that it possesses the first, it denies the second and completely disrupts its proper relation to the state. Through the second temptation the church can be so blinded that it mistakes those things which are purely external and accidental to its nature for what is essential and necessary and so becomes entangled with the state to whose essence those externals really do belong. From this angle, then, the perduring maxims for church politics are humility and indifference to earthly possessions; this is a political program which, I think, suits the church well.

#347

The church cannot directly and immediately prevent the state's trespassing beyond its proper sphere, for these are acts of force, and the state's force is not subject to the church. But if this happened, if the state tried to arrogate to itself dominion over consciences by establishing a creed and worship and an organized church, or if it pretended to introduce changes in them through state measures, if it regarded the church as an arm of the state and treated it as such, then the church would be in danger of becoming subservient to the state's ends and of being enslaved and perhaps destroyed by it. Since the principle of self-preservation is universal, ecclesiastical politics must insure, first of all, that on the church's part no occasion is given for such an intrusion of the state and then that, should there be threat of such an intrusion, it can be repelled by suitable means.

> * Prudent church governance has, in the very temptations which it must fear within itself, clear indications of when it has to fear danger from the state. If a spirit of domination awakens in the ruling power of the state and, instead of confining itself to the larger interests of the nation, it intrudes upon individuals and into people's private affairs, then inevitably it will run up against religion and the church. Furthermore, if the state's needs—always the source of problems—leads to a hunger for possessions, those things which are extrinsic to the church—its goods—will certainly not be spared, since they are in fact separable

from what is intrinsic to the church. But in the course of despoiling the church of those extrinsic possessions the despoiling hand will inevitably do violence to what is intrinsic to it. —The unprejudiced student of history knows full well to what periods these and the preceding remarks apply and that what occurs in one age is a reaction to what has occurred in another.

#348

Should the state overstep its bounds, prudent church government has no other means of restoring the proper relationship which has been destroyed save those by which the church constantly maintains its existence within the state, namely, openness and conciliation. These means, based on its internal autonomy and independence, it tries to make respected, and the notion of concordats, which first appeared in the theory of church polity (#307), finds its realization in church governance. This introduction has to derive the principles and rules for negotiating them from this theory.

> * Concordats are definitions of limits between the domains of state and church by which free action within both is mutually guaranteed; they are the pivotal points around which both remain in balance with one another. Since they are always formulated in and for a particular time, they are always of a temporary character and so a kind of occasional expedient. But anyone wanting to disparage them for that reason would also have to insist that everything within the life of the church and of the state remains always and forever static.

#349

Nevertheless, prudent church governance cannot assure the church's well-being by openness and conciliation alone. For this balance is temporary and can always be upset once again. It can never, or at least not for a very long time yet, achieve its final rest. Before this happens, the church will find itself in times of duress, and if the church's government had no other means of defense, then the church would be lost. Outwardly the church depends on openness and conciliation, but inwardly it relies exclusively on its spirit; if this is powerful and of the right kind, then the church may be certain of withstanding any external persecution, relying on the fact that spiritual force is greater than physical force and will prove victorious.

Therefore, at all times the most pressing concern of church government must be to purify and strengthen the church's spirit.

> * Thus, from this angle, the maxims for church politics are outward love of peace and inward strength of spirit, and in my opinion, these political positions should cause no statesman anxiety.

2. Introduction to Church Administration or to Church Ministry

#350

If the work of church government is exercised on the church as a whole or on the church in its largest divisions, the work of church administration or church ministry, by contrast, is exercised on particular areas and particular persons; the basic community of persons is the *parish*. The shape of the church comes from the shape of the parish; leadership in the church culminates in leadership of the parish.

#351

But for this very reason the pastoral charge is entirely subordinate to the church's government and is dependent upon it for the individuals under its pastoral guidance, for the precepts and norms in accord with which they are guided, and for the elements of church life which take on practical life through pastoral guidance. The subjects of this charge, the authority and the prescriptions for its use are given to administrative officers by the church's governors. Consequently, they are called *ministers of the church*. Although to this extent the work of a minister of the church is limited, it is still free and autonomous in terms of the precise way he performs it and the means by which he attempts to make it as fruitful as possible. What such a minister is required to do in his office can be prescribed for him, but how he can perform it in the best and most effective way is up to his own decision and to the training which is called an introduction to church ministry—or also *the care of souls*.

#352

Thus the work of the church's ministers has the parish as the object of its special attention. As the parish can be thought of either as a unit or as the individual members who make it up, so the minister's attention can be directed either directly to the whole parish (as a congregation) or indirectly through the care of souls undertaken for individual members but with reference to the whole. The first is the public, the second the private care of souls. Pastoral theology must provide instruction for the fulfillment of one's duties in both.

#353

The guidelines which this introduction can provide must be derived from the general goals of all pastoral work and from the special nature of each kind of work. The general goal of all pastoral action is the direct and explicit realization of the ideas of Christianity in each individual believer, or the awakening and nourishing of spiritual life in Christ within the members of his church. What distinguishes a particular pastoral action is that it does this in its own peculiar way by working through some one element of the church's life as its medium and making this element especially vital in individuals. Just as the elements of the church's life are doctrine, worship, and church discipline (##291, 292, 293) and the mission of church government is to preserve and clarify them, so in complementary fashion the mission of the church's ministry is to convey these elements of the church's life to individuals, to root them in those individuals, and to make them fruitful for the lives of those individuals and for the whole church. All this can be summarized in three responsibilities, and there are thus three forms of pastoral action.

#354

The church's minister is first of all a *teacher of Christianity* in the name of the church, and his first responsibility toward the parish is to give instruction in Christian doctrine both theoretically as religious teaching and practically as moral teaching. And, of course, this instruction will seek to bring about both full commitment within the mind and lively affection within the heart.

#355

This introduction can be divided both in regard to its breadth and completeness in content and in regard to its form of presentation. The first of these regards creates the distinction between an elementary and a more detailed instruction depending on the audience's intellectual abilities; the second leads to a distinction between elegant and simple forms of address depending subjectively on the style of the speaker and objectively on the purpose of the speech.

#356

Whenever one talks of education the understanding is obviously involved. The teaching offered by the minister of the church aimed at instruction in Christianity is called *catechesis*, and the minister in question is a *catechist*. With respect to the recipient's intellectual ability catechesis is divided into *elementary catechesis* for children and catechumens, in the sense of that term as the ancient church used it, and *advanced catechesis* for those who are already members of the congregation. This latter can easily take on the form of an actual lecture—a *catechetical lecture*.

> * Since the person who still needs elementary instruction in Christianity cannot be considered an actual member of the Christian community, even though he may have some claim to this status since for centuries the ancient church so regarded him, elementary catechesis, or catechesis properly so-called, is not part of the minister's official instruction work or of his official pastoral duties; but catechetical lectures are.

#357

Besides education, whenever there is question of emotion and stirring lively religious affections one is preeminently involved with the heart, and the minister's style of speech becomes *oratory*. The official oratory of the church's minister aimed especially at the affections and religious enthusiasm of the congregation is called *preaching*, and the minister in question is a *preacher*. To perform his task the preacher may rely on his own religious enthusiasm and natural talent for striking speech or turn for assistance to training in the arts of rhetoric. In the first case he is a *simple* preacher, in the second a *technically trained* one.

> * Preaching and catechesis belong among the clergy's first responsibilities to the parish, and although regarded as teaching and instruction, they are really acts of worship aimed not so much at teaching as at the affections—because religious affection is conditioned by teaching. Catechetical instruction interprets acts of worship especially, and preaching

serves the religious affection which it at the same time excites and the more definite forms into which it develops and is channeled.

#358

Because education in Christianity can be considered a part of general education which has its own object and its own methods, the minister needs a suitable training for the fruitful discharge of this part of his office, and this training is *catechetics*. Thus, this is the first discipline within pastoral theology.

> *   So catechetics establishes the foundation for the ability gradually to bring the Christian principle within the heart to awareness and continually clearer vision, always with due regard, of course, for the difference between what is fixed and what is mutable in Christian doctrine (##256, 258), although in a simple manner proportioned to people's intellectual abilities.

#359

Likewise, it is understandable that the minister requires special training for the preaching office. Such training has been customarily given the name *homiletics*; it is the second discipline within pastoral theology.

> *   Homiletics has been variously evaluated in the past and still continues to be so evaluated. Some, to whom the pure spirit of Christianity was not only the central matter but all that matters, have denounced every admixture of oratorical art as alien, indeed as destructive; others, often as a result of secular tastes, have regarded those arts as indispensable and have even more often profaned the pulpit with vulgarity and worldliness. The truth of the matter is actually this: religious enthusiasm which goes beyond the rules of aesthetic good taste loses its impact; pulpit oratory which eschews religious enthusiasm ends up empty word-juggling. But when inner spiritual energy is united with the beauty of true art it irresistibly draws people's hearts.

#360

The second subject of the minister's public work is Christian worship. He has to lead it and to make it efficacious within the parish.

In this regard, he is called a *liturgist* or a *priest* in the usual sense of the word.

#361

The material of worship or its objective actions and forms is given to the minister by the church's government; of his own power, he can change nothing essential to it. But insofar as worship steps into the realm of religious art—which always keeps pace with the general level of artistic culture, so that the church's government can determine the forms of worship only in broad and general outline—it must be left up to the minister to make final decisions in particular cases and to avoid extreme products of unrestrained imaginations.

#362

But these decisions are not the minister's essential task as liturgist. His essential work is rather so to celebrate and supervise sacred acts of worship that the hearts of the faithful are moved to experience and feel in fact what the sensible forms mean symbolically. As liturgist, the minister consequently acts in a twofold character and double capacity: first, as a functionary of the church, as so to speak, its organ in the administration of worship, and then as a free being. In the first capacity his manner of acting is determined, in the second self-directed. Apart from the second, the first would be bare, spiritless, and mechanical; apart from the first, the second might indeed be a living, spirit-filled event, but not a manifestation of Christian ideas and not in their ecclesial form. The liturgist must therefore energize the mechanics of his functions as prescribed for him by the church and fill them with his own individual spiritual life.

#363

There can and must be special instruction in those mechanics. The minister receives that instruction in *liturgics*, which is thus the third among pastoral disciplines. It gives a thorough knowledge of ecclesiastical forms of worship, including their meaning and the way they are to be celebrated. As for the liturgist's individual and personal actions whereby he energizes his functions, no prescriptions can be provided; that is entirely up to his own religious devotion and his aesthetic sense.

#364

Finally, the work of the minister includes the administration of church discipline within his church. As in view of its internal and external structure the church establishes for expediency's sake certain statutory decisions as ecclesiastically binding (#293), it is the minister's task to exercise oversight and see to the practical execution of those ordinances in his parish. In this capacity he acts as a subordinate officer in the church and is a *rector* or *pastor*.

#365

Beyond knowledge of general disciplinary laws and the reasons they have been enacted, for the faithful performance of this part of the minister's office there is required both the special skill of interpreting legal prescriptions and a special prudence for which only the most general guidelines can be offered. The minister's education in this respect is dealt with in *pastoral skills* and in a training in pastoral prudence, which also deserves a place among the disciplines of pastoral theology. Since the minister's work in this regard tends always to deal more with mechanics and externals and to border on the limits of the secular, pastoral theology has to caution him against overstepping those limits and the minister himself has to demonstrate that same mind-set which he brings to all his other functions.

#366

The minister's activities are in no way exhausted by his responsibilities to his parish. For since these presume the existence and continuance of the parish community—and both the existence and continuance of the parish depend on the behavior of its individual members—the minister must exercise his care for the individual members of the parish and for their behavior toward the parish. Thus the minister is called a *guide of souls* or a *shepherd of souls*.

#367

The parish community's existence and continuance depend on the behavior of individuals, first, when the community reproduces itself through the individual members whom it joins to itself and with whom it replaces those who have departed, and second, when those individual members who have been accepted into the parish community act as worthy and active members, do not sever themselves from it, and do not incur any separation from church authority.

> * It is clear from this why, on the one hand, the cure of souls is necessary for the church's existence and continuance, and on the other hand, why all its responsibilities, although aimed at individuals, in fact concern the whole community and specifically unity with it.

#368

From this the responsibilities of the cure of souls can be defined and classified. They are all geared either toward introducing new members into the parish community, or toward holding within it those who through their errors are in danger of inwardly or outwardly separating from the community, or toward making what they are missing available by means of private edification to those who are prevented by physical causes from participating in the parish's spiritual activities. Thus the responsibilities of the cure of souls can be reduced to *catechizing, pastoral correction,* and *visiting the sick,* the aged, the imprisoned, etc.

#369

For these responsibilities the beginning pastor of souls requires training, and it is the task of personal pastoral theology to supply him with this. We have already discussed *catechetics* as a general training in imparting Christian instruction. Here the term refers to the special sense of training in the many aspects of preparing those who wish to become and deserve to be members of the community.

#370

Although as a rule these are children and their preparation is done in *children's classes,* cases do occasionally arise when non-Christians or Christians of another confession want to become members of the parish community. As preparation of such candidates has its own special requirements, the pastor of souls needs special training for it, and personal pastoral education deals with this under the name of *preparation of converts.*

#371

Pastoral correction has as its purpose the individual's good moral standing and tries to assist it by private encouragement and to restore it when it is threatened. In the latter case, the minister charged with the cure of souls demonstrates his skill as a *physician of souls*; this belongs among the most serious of his obligations and demands both attention and prudence.

#372

A diseased moral state in a person may have its cause either in the theoretical or the practical domain but most often in both. The pastor of souls must recognize that cause and counteract it either through private exhortation or through other ascetical means.

#373

This morally diseased state may originally be confined to a single person, but it can easily spread further as a result of temptation and evil example. Frequently it is spread through the various relations of common life, for example, through marriage, family, domestic relations, etc. The more contagious and epidemic this moral sickness becomes, the more energetically must the pastor of souls labor to counter it.

#374

Since by its moral principles Christianity makes admonishing sinners a duty of every member of the community, the pastor will not only refrain from hindering this personal correction but will recognize it as part of his pastoral wisdom to encourage it in appropriate circumstances when it may often be more suitable and more effective than pastoral correction. But he must supervise this and determine the occasions when it is necessary to permit this.

#375

The purpose of pastoral correction is always inner spiritual identity with the community. But there are cases when, after all other means have failed, the one and only recourse remaining is the severance of that identity even externally. The pastor tries to avoid this last resort as much as possible. From this it can be understood how necessary is his *training in pastoral correction* in all its dimensions and how important study of its theory is.

#376

It is easier to deal with those who are prevented from participating in the congregation's communal life due simply to some unintended accident and who, it may be presumed, as a rule have maintained their inner identity with the community. But it is the pastor's duty to guard lest these accidental sources of external separation undermine inner identity.

#377

The way of treating these people who have been unintentionally separated breaks down into two kinds of care: general care in which the pastor supports their religious life in the same way and through the same means as he cares for the community at large through his public functions, and special care in which he tries to protect against all harmful factors at work in their particular state and to turn that state into an opportunity to improve their religious life. —In a special branch of this introduction pastoral theology teaches him how to offer these two kinds of care.

#378

The obligations mentioned above define for him the task which the church has entrusted to him and for his performance of which he is answerable to it. But what his office and the church have not defined for him, because it cannot be defined, is a great number of delicate considerations and practical religious concerns in which he is engaged regarding both the whole community and each individual person. By the significance of his official position and the conditions under which it was entrusted to him he has already been set up as an example to the people around him of one who has been formed by the forces of the church's life into an authentically *religious person*, an example for all the faithful who are to model themselves on him. He must conduct himself as an example to the community and to every person in it in all the various situations in which one person may interact with others. Life in society is the arena of his general relationships, but he is involved in many special relationships because of the demands of his office and the expectations of the faithful. In all these relationships it is part of his vocation to awaken and support religious life in his parish through his own religious life even more than through the duties of his official position.

> * The life and the numerous and varied personal activities of the pastor must make real the abstract notion of his official character. He is only a genuine teacher when his life exemplifies what his lips preach. He is only an authentic priest when his whole being is seen as dedicated to the Holy—to God—and all his effort as devoted to the good of human beings—to the community. He is only a true shepherd and guide to holiness and sanctity when he not only knows the way but has walked it in advance of the others.

#379

This *subjective* expertise through which the clergy are able to labor most fruitfully in their office cannot be learned from, still less imparted by, any discipline of practical theology. It is the result of a higher consecration by the power of religion, preeminently by the power of that love for God and humanity which is supposed to be the practical principle of the Christian religion. Only to one who fosters this power within himself and with its support strives earnestly toward his lofty goal will *pastoral ascetics* and *pastoral techniques* geared to this aforementioned goal be of any use. By themselves they are only mechanical means. Therefore, when someone is inwardly transformed, seeks to live rightly, and brings his inner drives under control, outwardly being an example and encouragement follows automatically. When the inner works of the clock are sound, the hands always point to the right time.

3. Study of Practical Theology

#380

Because the church's mission—in church government and ministry—presumes knowledge of the means and norms by which the mission can and ought to be accomplished (#326), it is dependent on a body of knowledge, and so the two introductions within practical theology form special disciplines. But as *practical* disciplines which simply teach how to apply what is already known (from other disciplines), they must borrow their fundamental principles from other more general and theoretical sciences. And so the question here is to indicate whence they take these fundamental principles and with what other studies practical theology must be connected.

#381

Since the essence of every act of church governance and ministry is the care of souls, and since consequently the basic principles of the introductions to both can only be the basic principles of the care of souls (#329), the most general principles of practical theology must be borrowed from *psychology*. Thus practical theology must, first of all, be familiar—or must become familiar—with that philosophical discipline. But since the care of souls is guided solely by religious motives and effected by religious means, it must especially be acquainted with the psychological laws by which religious dispositions develop in the human soul and the principles by which external factors can assist that development.

#382

In its most general form the clergy's task within the church is education (#73), and even in their external role within the state they are public educators. Their practical formation must therefore be *pedagogical*; they cannot remain unacquainted with the basic principles of the science of education. They must be familiar with them generally and, because of the crucial purpose of the education they impart, must know especially how they can be applied to people's religious education.

#383

Because the church is an ethical state, a Kingdom of God, and church government on the global level and ministry on the local level labor to establish it visibly in the world (##324, 328), and if with Schleiermacher we designate as *ethics* the general science dealing with the principles by which ideas necessarily innate within human nature are shaped by history and form societies and cultures,[39] then anyone charged with leadership in the church must know those principles especially. To the degree that his work in the governance of the church is not blind and unconscious but is established on a scientific basis, he must abstract from those principles of ethics his theory of church governance and politics (#332). And although here again what has been repeatedly noted about narrowing universal principles to special areas—in this case, religion—remains true, yet in the church as an outward phenomenon the special area—religion—actually becomes the universal. —What has just been said also applies to the minister, only in a more restricted field.

> * These are the *general* principles and sciences from which practical theology and all who wish to gain a thorough knowledge of it must derive its foundations. Special knowledge and principles are required for the duties of a minister in which a pastoral theology designed for him will provide instruction.

#384

Certainly it can readily be seen that the basic principles and rules of pedagogy are absolutely essential, especially for the exercise of his teaching office. The successful performance of the office of a Christian teacher, whether in its public or private exercise (homiletics, catechetics), must be built on these principles. Such a *pastoral pedagogy* with its principles and examples becomes all the more essential now, when the ones to be instructed stand for the most part on a noticeably lower educational level and the one who is to instruct, because of his course of education and the present situation of theology, is even more removed from their way of thinking. Thus the teacher-to-be requires special instruction in how to instruct people on anything and how to communicate effectively to them the positive doctrines of religion.

> * While this pedagogy provides the basis for catechesis and ordinary homiletics, the teacher of religion who wants to elevate his speaking to the heights of inspired oratory, agreeable to time and circumstances and to his own and his audience's needs, cannot forego being trained in the rules of the sacred art. Pulpit oratory belongs among the fields of study within practical theology. Yet even now both its guidelines and examples are rare commodities, especially among us Germans.

#385

If liturgics is to be more than mere empirical knowledge of rituals and rubrics, which can certainly be very easily achieved with very little thought, it must be based on the science of art. Only through a religious aesthetic sense and a religious aesthetic taste can the church leader be properly trained to evaluate currently existing liturgical forms and to organize new ones. And only under the same proviso will the minister as the actual liturgist correctly celebrate and explain unusual aspects of worship. But in practice the same situation prevails here as with pulpit oratory.

#386

The studies mentioned here include those principles which provide the scientific basis for the various kinds of training which practical theology provides the clergy. But just as practical theology cannot be exhaustively defined either by scientific principles or by rules derived from them, so for many readily understandable reasons this is most particularly true of the practicum for the exercise of the clerical office. Consequently, so-called pastoral theologians have in their courses of instruction always left open a place for *pastoral wisdom* as something indefinable by prescriptions. For what one encounters here and there in handbooks under the name of rules of *pastoral prudence* is actually concerned only with what might be called routine instances and may occasionally be a useful guide for the inept but can just as often and easily be used ineptly by them.

#387

There is thus no training in pastoral wisdom. Viewed inwardly, it is the product of a well-formed mind and heart, viewed outwardly, the fruit of experience guided by reflection. So we can only indicate what underlies it. In one who has become scientifically knowledgeable about the state of Christianity and of the church, especially in his own day, in one who unites to this knowledge a deep commitment, an undivided will, reverence and zeal for his office, and further does not leave outside his notice the age in which and the people among whom he lives, in him the wisdom of a shepherd of the church and a guide of souls develops naturally and increases daily.

#388

But what of the education provided by practical theology and the various principles and fields of knowledge which it presumes (##381–386) pertains to the mastery of some particular role is fairly well determined by the way practical theology is divided up and by the clear division of clerical offices and responsibilities in our church. One charged with leadership in the church must have special knowledge of whatever education shows to be necessary for the exercise of church governance; one charged with ministry in the church must have knowledge of whatever it designates as necessary for church administration. Since, however, the church leader also oversees church administration and the minister acts in the spirit of the church's government, each must be well-versed in the other's area of responsibility.

TRANSLATOR'S NOTES

1. Gottlieb Jakob Planck (1751–1833) taught theology and church history at Göttingen from 1784. He described his own theological position as "rational supernaturalism," the assumption that revelation is essentially attainable by the right use of reason. The work to which Drey refers here is his *Grundriss der theologischen Enzyklopädie* (Göttingen, 1813).

2. Friedrich Daniel Ernst Schleiermacher (1768–1834) taught at Halle (1804–1807) and then at the new university of Berlin from 1810 until his death. His encyclopedia was the *Kurze Darstellung des theologischen Studiums zum Behuf einleitender Vorlesungen*; see Introduction, n. 18.

3. In 1819, when the *Brief Introduction* was published, Drey had been teaching his course in theological encyclopedia for seven years.

4. Desiderius Erasmus of Rotterdam (c. 1469–1536), the famous humanist, was the author of the *Enchiridion militis christianae* and the Μωρίας Ἐγκώμιον, *seu Laus Stultitiae*, the editor of the Greek text of the New Testament, and opponent of Luther on the question of the freedom of the will.

5. Philipp Schwarzerd (1497–1560), known as Melanchthon, was Luther's friend and supporter and the most humanistic of the early Reformers. His *Loci communes* (1st ed. 1521) was the first summary of Reformation doctrine.

6. Jean le Charlier de Gerson (1363–1429), the so-called "doctor christianissimus" and noted defender of conciliarism, was chancellor of the University of Paris from 1395–1415.

7. Nicholas Poillevillain of Clémanges or Clamanges (1367–1437), a friend of Gerson and conciliarist theorist, insisted on the need for a pastoral orientation in theology in his *De studio theologico*.

8. Jean Luc d'Achery (1609–1685), librarian of St. Germain-des-Prés, wrote the thirteen volumes of his *Spicilegium veterum aliquot scriptorum qui in Galliae bibliothecis, maxime Benedictinorum, latuerant* between 1655 and 1677.

9. Johann Salomo Semler (1725–1791), noted biblical critic, taught theology at Halle from 1753 to 1791.

10. François Annat (1590–1670), Jesuit theologian who taught at Toulouse from 1648 until 1652 and subsequently became Louis XIV's confessor, was a determined opponent of Jansenism. Pascal addressed the seventeenth and eighteenth of his *Lettres provinciales* to him.

11. Antonio Possevino (1534–1611) was a Jesuit diplomat, scriptural scholar, and anti-Protestant polemicist.

12. Jean Mabillon (1632–1707), great Benedictine scholar, assisted d'Achery in compiling the *Spicilegium*, wrote a monumental history of the Benedictine order and was an early liturgical historian.

13. Louis-Ellies Du Pin (1657–1719), Jansenist theologian and Gallican canonist, was an early proponent of ecumenical reunion between Roman Catholicism, Orthodoxy, and Anglicanism. His chief work was his *Bibliothèque universelle des auteurs ecclésiastiques* in sixty-one volumes. His *Méthode pour étudier la théologie* was published in 1716.

14. Andreas Gerhard (1511–1564), known as Hyperius, was a Lutheran Reformer and theologian. His principal work was *De ratione studii theologici* of 1556.

15. Georg Calixt or Calixtus (1586–1656) was the most important continuator of Lutheran theology in the line of Melanchthon. He was an influential scriptural exegete and an early advocate of ecumenism.

16. Johann Franz Budde (Johannes Franciscus Buddeus; 1667–1729) taught philosophy at Wittenberg, Jena, and Halle and, for a brief time, classical languages at Coburg. Regarded as the most learned of German religious thinkers in his time, he published more than one hundred works in his lifetime. The *Isagoge historico-theologica ad theologiam universam* (1st ed. 1727) was an exceptionally progressive treatment of theological encyclopedia.

17. Christoph Matthaeus Pfaff (1686–1760), Lutheran theologian of Pietist leanings at Tübingen and chancellor of the university for thirty-six years, wrote many works of varying interest and value. He was a noted biblical scholar but was not above altering and even forging texts.

18. Johann Georg Walch (1693–1775) taught philosophy and theology at Jena. He edited Luther's collected works and was an indefatigable collector of theological source materials. Drey referred to him as the "elder" to distinguish him from his son, Christian Wilhelm Franz Walch (1726–1784), who succeeded his father in the chair of philosophy at Jena and later taught at Göttingen.

19. Stephan Wiest (1748–1797), a Cistercian, was a disciple of Johann Michael Sailer and professor of dogmatics at Ingolstadt.

20. See n. 19.

21. Franz Oberthür (1745–1831) taught dogmatics, history of dogmatics and polemics at Würzburg; like Drey, he criticized scholastic theology and emphasized the importance of history and biblical exegesis for theology.

22. Franz Xaver Gmeiner (1752–1824) was an Austrian canonist and church historian of a strongly Josephinist cast at the university of Graz.

23. Johann August Nösselt (1734–1807) taught theology at the university of Halle; his *Anweisung zur Bildung angehender Theologen* was first published in two volumes in 1785.

24. See n. 1.

25. Johann Gottfried Herder (1744–1803), the great German litterateur and philosopher, wrote his *Briefe, das Studium der Theologie betreffend* in 1780–81 in Weimar. The letters were intended as a practical guide for theology students.

26. Johann Friedrich Wilhelm Thym (1768–1803) taught theology at Halle.

27. Johann August Heinrich Tittman (1773–1831) first taught philosophy and later theology at Leipzig. He held to a rational supernaturalism similar to that of Planck.

28. Johann Ernst Christian Schmidt (1772–1831) taught at Giessen; he is primarily remembered today as a pioneer of the higher criticism of the New Testament.

29. Marian Dobmayer (1753–1805) was a Benedictine theologian who taught philosophy at Neuburg and subsequently dogmatics and church history at Amberg and Ingolstadt. The work to which Drey refers eventually reached eight volumes by the time of its complete posthumous publication in 1819.

30. Karl Daub (1765–1836) began his teaching career in theology at Marburg and then taught for many years at Heidelberg. His thought went through several distinct stages as he moved from Kant's influence to that of Schelling and finally to a Hegelian position.

31. See n. 2.

32. Franz Ignatz Thanner (1770–1825) wrote several encyclopedic works. Although some of his later works showed the influence of Schelling, in his *Einleitung zum akademisch-wissenschaftlichen Studium der positiven Theologie* he emphasized the importance of the idea of the Kingdom of God but interpreted it in the heavily moralistic sense typical of the *Aufklärung*.

33. These lectures are entitled "On the Historical Construction of Christianity" and "On Theology," pp. 80–99; see Introduction, n. 26.

34. See #81 (2) and n. 4.

35. Schelling's Third Lecture is entitled "On the First Presuppositions of Academic Study," pp. 33–41; see Introduction, n. 26.

36. The reference is to *Kurze Darstellung*, 1st ed., p. 36, #15; Scholz, ed., p. 47, n.1.

37. The reference is to *Kurze Darstellung*, 1st ed., p. 39, #27; Scholz, ed., p. 53, n. 2.

38. See n. 27.

39. The reference is to *Kurze Darstellung*, passim., esp. 1st ed., p. 12, #6; Scholz, ed., p. 15, n. 1.

SELECTED BIBLIOGRAPHY

Drey's Work

Books

Observata quaedam ad illustrandam Justini martyris de regno millenaria sententiam. Gamundiae: Typis Joann. Georg. Ritter, 1814.

Dissertatio historico-theologica originem et vicissitudinem exomologeseos in ecclesia catholica ex documentis ecclesiasticis illustrans. Ellwangen: Typis Joann. Georg. Ritter, 1815.

Kurze Einleitung in das Studium der Theologie mit Rücksicht auf den wissenschaftlichen Standpunkt und das katholische System von Dr. Johann Sebastian Drey, Professor der Theologie an der katholischen Fakultät in Tübingen. Tübingen: Heinrich Laupp, 1819; repr. Frankfurt: Minerva, 1966; also Darmstadt: Wissenschaftliche Buchgesellschaft, 1971.

Neue Untersuchungen über die Constitutionen und kanones der Apostel. Tübingen: Heinrich Laupp, 1832. Originally published in *Theologische Quartalschrift* 11 (1829): 397–477, 609–723, as "Über die apostolischen Konstitutionen, oder neue Untersuchungen über die Bestandteile, Entstehung und Zusammensetzung und den kirchlichen Wert dieser alten Schrift."

Die Apologetik als wissenschaftliche Nachweisung der Göttlichkeit des Christentums in seiner Erscheinung, dargestellt von Dr. Johann Sebastian v. Drey. 3 vols. Mainz: Fl. Kupferberg, vol. 1, 1838; vol. 2, 1843; vol. 3, 1847. Reprinted Frankfurt: Minerva, 1967.

Articles

"Revision des gegenwärtigen Zustandes der Theologie." *Archiv für die Pastoralkonferenzen in Landkapiteln des Bistums Konstanz* (1812) 1:3–26. Reprinted in Josef Rupert Geiselmann, ed., *Geist des Christentums und des Katholizismus. Ausgewählte Schriften katholischer Theologie im Zeitalter des deutschen Idealismus und der Romantik*, 83-97. Mainz: Matthias Grünewald, 1940. Also in Franz Schupp, ed., *Johann Sebastian Drey: Revision von Kirche und Theologie, Drei Aufsätze*, 1–24. Darmstadt: Wissenschaftliche Buchgesellschaft, 1971.

"Vom Geist und Wesen des Katholizismus." *Theologischen Quartalschrift* 1 (1819): 8–23, 193–210, 369–391, and 559–574. Reprinted in Geiselmann, ed., *Geist des Christentums*, pp. 195–234.

"Grundsätze zu einer genaueren Bestimmung des Begriffs der Inspiration." *Theologische Quartalschrift* 2 (1820): 387–411 and 3 (1821): 230–261, 615–655.

"Über das Kirchengebot, Ostern nie mit den Juden zu halten." *Theologische Quartalschrift* 2 (1820): 626–636.

"Ehrerbietige Wünsche und Andeutungen in Bezug auf Verbesserungen in der katholischen Kirchenzucht, zunächst in Deutschland." *Theologische Quartalschrift* 4 (1822): 225–259.

"Über die Predigt als Bestandteil der öffentlichen Gottesverehrung in der katholischen Kirche." *Theologische Quartalschrift* 4 (1822): 403–424.

"Der katholische Lehrsatz von der Gemeinschaft der Heiligen, aus seiner Idee und seiner Anwendung auf verschiedene andere Lehrpunkte dargestellt." *Theologische Quartalschrift* 4 (1822): 587–634. Reprinted in Geiselmann, ed., *Geist des Christentums*, pp. 359–388.

"Über den Satz von der allein seligmachenden Kirche." In J. Graz, ed., *Der Apologet des Katholizismus*, 5: 39–85. Mainz: 1822. Reprinted in Geiselmann, ed., *Geist des Christentums*, pp. 336–357.

"Über das Verhältnis des Mystizismus zum Katholizismus, mit Nutzanwendung für unsere Zeit." *Theologische Quartalschrift* 6 (1824): 219–248. Reprinted in Schupp, ed., *Revision von Kirche und Theologie*, pp. 25–54.

"Über Kirchenstrafen als Beförderungsmittel der Sittlichkeit und ihre Anwendung in unserer Zeit." *Theologische Quartalschrift* 6 (1824): 583–621.

"Aphorismen über den Ursprung unserer Erkenntnisse von Gott—ein Beitrag zur Entscheidung der neuesten Streitigkeiten über den Begriff der Offenbarung." *Theologische Quartalschrift* 8 (1826): 237–284.

"Über Proselyten und Proselytenmachen." *Theologische Quartalschrift* 8 (1826): 622–666.

"Von der Landesreligion und der Weltreligion." *Theologische Quartalschrift* 9 (1827): 234–274, 391–435.

"Der Schreiber in der Kirche." *Theologische Quartalschrift* 11 (1829): 38–75.

"Von der Verhältnissen der nichtunierten griechischen Kirche in den oesterreichischen Staaten." *Theologische Quartalschrift* 11 (1829): 195–250.

"Über die Anwendung weltlicher Regierungsweisen auf die Regierung der Kirche." *Theologische Quartalschrift* 13 (1831): 1–43.

"Über die Öffentliche und liturgische Beichten." *Theologische Quartalschrift* 14 (1832): 494–525.

"Was ist in unserer Zeit von Synoden zu erwarten?" *Theologische Quartalschrift* 16 (1834): 203–256.

"Über die bei Anordnung neuer Rituale zu beachtenden Grundsätze, mit Rücksicht auf das neue Ritual der Erzdiözese Freiburg." *Theologische Quartalschrift* 17 (1835): 585–623.

"Über Lesevereine der Geistlichen, deren Zweck, Einrichtung und Leitung." *Theologische Quartalschrift* 22 (1840): 75–102.

"Die rückläufige Bewegung im Protestantismus und ihre Bedeutung." *Theologische Quartalschrift* 26 (1844): 3–56.

Posthumously published

"Geschichte des katholischen Dogmensystems. I. Band. Geschichte der drei ersten Jahrhunderte oder erste Periode. Mit Benutzung von Münschers Handbuch dargestellt von Dr. J. S. Drey Pr. 1812–1813." Published as "Ideen zur Geschichte des katholischen Dogmensystems." In Geiselmann, ed., *Geist des Christentums*, pp. 235–331.

"Mein Tagebuch über philosophische, theologische und historische Gegenstände, enthaltend Auszüge, Rezensionen und eigene Bermerkungen und beifällige Ideen. . . ." Excerpts published in Geiselmann, ed., *Geist des Christentums*, pp. 99–192.

Works on Drey

Burtchaell, James Tunstead. "Drey, Möhler and the Catholic School of Tübingen." In *Nineteenth-Century Religious Thought in the West*, 3 vols., ed. Ninian Smart, John Clayton, Patrick Sherry, and Steven T. Katz, 2:111–139. Cambridge: Cambridge University Press, 1985.

Fehr, Wayne L. *The Birth of the Catholic Tübingen School: The Dogmatics of Johann Sebastian Drey.* American Academy of Religion Academy Series 37. Chico, Calif.: Scholars Press, 1981.

Geiselmann, Josef Rupert. "Die Glaubenswissenschaft der katholischen Tübinger Schule in ihrer Grundlegung durch Johann Sebastian von Drey." *Theologische Quartalschrift* 111 (1930): 49–117.

———. *Die Katholische Tübinger Schule: Ihre theologische Eigenart.* Freiburg: Herder, 1964.

Himes, Michael J. "Historical Theology as *Wissenschaft*: Johann Sebastian Drey and the Structure of Theology." In *Revisioning the Past: Prospects in Historical Theology*, ed. Mary Potter Engel and Walter E. Wyman, Jr., pp. 191–213. Minneapolis: Fortress Press, 1992.

O'Meara, Thomas Franklin. *Romantic Idealism and Roman Catholicism: Schelling and the Theologians.* Notre Dame: University of Notre Dame Press, 1982. See esp. pp. 94–108.

Rief, Josef, "Johann Sebastian von Drey (1777-1853)." In *Katholische Theolo-*

gen Deutschlands im 19. Jahrhundert. 3 vols., ed. Heinrich Fries and Georg Schwaiger, 2: 9–39. Munich: Kösel-Verlag, 1975.

———. *Reich Gottes und Gesellschaft nach Johann Sebastian Drey und Johann Baptist Hirscher.* Paderborn: F. Schöningh, 1965.

Ruf, Wolfgang. *Johann Sebastian von Dreys System der Theologie als Begründung der Moraltheologie.* Studien zur Theologie und Geistesgeschichte des Neunzehnten Jahrhunderts, Bd. 7. Göttingen: Vandenhoeck und Ruprecht, 1974.

Schupp, Franz. *Die Evidenz der Geschichte: Theologie als Wissenschaft bei J. S. Drey.* Innsbrück: Universität Innsbrück im Kommissionsverlag der Österreichischen Kommissionsbuchhandlung, 1970.

Thiel, John E. "J. S. Drey on Doctrinal Development: The Context of Theological Encyclopedia." *Heythrop Journal* 27, no. 3 (July 1986): 290–305.

———. "Theological Responsibility: Beyond the Classical Paradigm." *Theological Studies* 47, no.4 (December 1986): 573–598.

About the Author and Translator

Johann Sebastian Drey (1777–1853) was Professor of Theology in the Catholic faculty at Tübingen, Germany. Rev. Michael J. Himes received his Doctorate of Philosophy in the History of Christianity from the University of Chicago with distinction in 1981. Currently Associate Professor of Theology at Boston College, Himes is the co-author of *Fullness of Faith: The Public Significance of Theology*.

BX
895
.D7413
1994
38789s